SCIENCE,
MYTH,
REALITY

SCIENCE, MYTH, REALITY

The Black Family in One-Half Century of Research

ELEANOR ENGRAM

Contributions in Afro-American and African Studies, Number 64

GREENWOOD PRESS
Westport, Connecticut • London, England

Library of Congress Cataloging in Publication Data

Engram, Eleanor.
  Science, myth, reality.

  (Contributions in Afro-American and African
studies, ISSN 0069-9624 ; no. 64)
    Includes bibliographical references and index.
    1. Afro-American families. I. Title. II. Series.
E185.86.E53   306.8′08996073   81-1262
ISBN 0-313-22835-3 (lib. bdg.)   AACR2

Library of Congress Catalog Card Number: 81-1262
ISBN: 0-313-22835-3
ISSN: 0069-9624

First published in 1982

Greenwood Press
A division of Congressional Information Service, Inc.
88 Post Road West, Westport, Connecticut 06881

Printed in the United States of America

10 9 8 7 6 5 4 3 2 1

To future black families who will find, when
confronted with the contradictions of the present,
sustaining values from their past.

With all of our just flouting of White convention and Black religion, some things remain eternally so—Birth, Death, Pain, Mating, Children, Age. Ever and anon, we must point at these truths and if the pointing be beautiful with music and ceremony or bare with silence and darkness—what matter? The width or narrowness of the gesture is a matter of choice.

W. E. Burghardt Du Bois
Crisis, June 1928

Contents

Illustration and Tables

Preface

Despite the breadth of concern implied by the title, *Science, Myth, Reality* examines just one narrow issue of concern to contemporary social science. Indirectly, it raises questions about the broader concepts of science, myth, and reality, especially as the lines distinguishing these concepts seem to blur where black families are being considered.

By *science* I refer to social science, although the paradigm upon which social scientific inquiry is based is the same found in so-called hard sciences, like physics, chemistry, and biology. That is, physical science, too, has its assumptions, theories, propositions, and hypotheses that provide the frameworks within which the answers are sought.

By *myth* I mean the institutionalized beliefs that unfold as truth, often without empirical validity.

Reality is perhaps the most difficult to define since it varies with perspectives influenced by the location of any individual in time and space. I define reality as that which is true to any individual or group of individuals and which may be independent of other truths that are evident to those at other locations in time and space.

Science, Myth, Reality reflects my sense of their interaction, of their unities and disunities. Thus, the fact that the world was considered flat in 1490, that it was documented as such by cartographers, and that oceans were traveled and negotiated accordingly is, at once, science, myth, and reality.

Although black families inhabit the globe, this work refers to black families in the United States only. There is some evidence of a Pan-American perspective on black families, if not an applicable global perspective.[1] Many of the popular and scientific explanations of black families in the United States correspond to those used to describe black families in other parts of the Americas—in Peru, in Cuba, and in the Carribean.[2]

Even within the United States there is no monolithic black family. In fact, there is as much variation *within* black America as there is between black and white America.[3] This variety is not, however, an aspect of the Afro-American reality that has been generally understood. I hope that this book will help to promote such a broader understanding.

The black family as employed herein is a construct used to describe the primary social networks in which the descendants of African slaves brought to North America are born, are nurtured, develop their identities, mate, and reproduce. These families are therefore: (1) families of orientation, that is, families within which one is socialized or brought up; (2) families of procreation, wherein one is a family leader with one's own mate and perhaps children; and (3) families of interaction, which include all of the above, as well as kin and nonkin who are primary in one's life and who in some fashion fulfill familial functions, including: nurturance, shelter, protection, sexual gratification, emotional gratification, identification, and reproduction.

The black families discussed in this book are usually coterminous with households, and related by blood or marriage, but not all black families are so. What is unifying in the experience of black families is that somewhere in their history, despite the gains they may have made, is racial discrimination and hostility. There are few black Americans who can attest to experiencing no racism. At whatever level we blacks function, we wear our skin like an "ebony letter." It distinguishes us and evokes for the perceiver the stereotypes associated with being black in the United States. And like Hawthorne's tragic heroine who wore the "A" for her adultery, we are subject to the conscious and unconscious denigration that flows from being patent and obvious members of a group designated as inferior.[4] Black families, of whatever hue, social class, or resource have helped their members to negotiate these social impediments to healthy development.

This work does not presume to have covered all of the research literature generated by interest in the black U.S. family, since such literature has appeared since the turn of the century and in many and varied fields of interest.

Historians have been concerned with the historical antecedents to contemporary family patterns. Anthropologists have been concerned with black families as cultural or subcultural configurations, or both. Psychologists have focused primarily on the intellectual and emotional development of young members, and sociologists have focused primarily on social structural concerns, including family roles, functions, statuses, and power.

In an effort to synthesize and extend the field, I have, I believe, covered significantly more of the research material than has been covered in any single source published to date. Most of the research done thus far has addressed a limited set of questions about black families, and each researcher, in concentrating on a specific area of concern, has synthesized only the literature that has been specifically relevant to that topic. Consequently, there has been no broad synthesis and methodological study of black family literature as is presented herein.

Much of the black family literature of this century has been in response to the theoretical atmosphere created by the government's publication of the Moynihan report in 1965 and so is concerned with the etiology of black traits and characteristics that have been termed pathological.[5] This kind of literature makes a broad work such as this a critical necessity, since conclusions garnered in research on black families will often be considered in policymaking arenas. The literature which is given credence through citation by other scholars and researchers should, therefore, be able to withstand scrupulously scientific scrutiny.

In this work, I have used the "snowball" approach. That is, I have referred to the primary studies cited by other researchers to assess the validity of the conclusions drawn from them. I have used this assessment technique within the theoretical contexts provided by the fields of family and black family studies as well as within the context of the very most recent research and historical revision. In addition, I have rummaged the archives of Atlanta University to uncover the primary work of some of the earliest black scholars concerned with black families (W. E. B. Du Bois and Charles Spurgeon Johnson, for example) in order to incorporate their very significant contributions to this field.

Having examined the *primary* research literature, I am left with much satisfaction, particularly with having gained intimate and extensive knowledge of the empirical status of black families.

NOTES

1. A. J. R. Russell-Wood, "The Black Family in the Americas." *Societas.* 8(1): 1-38. 1978.

2. Ibid.

3. James E. Blackwell, *The Black Community: Diversity and Unity.* New York: Harper and Row. 1975.

4. In Nathaniel Hawthorne's *Scarlet Letter*, Hester Prynne wore the letter *A*, cut from red cloth and embroidered in gold, on the breast of her gown. The letter symbolized her having committed adultery. See S. Bradley, R. C. Beatty, and E. H. Long, eds., *The American Tradition in Literature.* Third edition. New York: Grosset and Dunlap. 1967.

5. Daniel Patrick Moynihan, *The Negro Family: The Case for National Action.* Washington, D.C.: U.S. Government Printing Office. 1965.

Acknowledgments

Those whom I thank for the development of this work are many. Some lie in a dimension of reality yet unexperienced by me. My father, Charlie Engram, of Georgia and Philadelphia, my grandmother, Mamie Brown, my pastor, Dr. William H. Gray, Jr., all deceased, each was and continues to be a source of encouragement and support. They planted many of the seeds of thought which have blossomed in this work.

My mother, Louise Engram, my aunts, Dorothy Holden and Eleanor Brown, my uncles, Albert, Earl, George, and Harold Brown, each played very special roles in this work, primarily by just being who they are and by lovingly supporting me and validating my work.

Throughout the fabric of my life run threads of family, woven with a loom of love, support, and encouragement. Miss Kelly, Aunt Fanny Welcher, Aunt Amy Brown, and the woman who first mothered my child as her own, and who now mothers my mother as her own, Beulah (Peggy) Garret—all were mothers to me and to my child. Sisters, (Play), Pearl Battle Simpson and Enola McCoy, on whom my child could unburden herself safely, and who would neither violate that trust nor take advantage of it, are as responsible for the completion of this work as I am.

Extending into the future the values of those aforementioned are my daughter, Janice P. Granby, and her daughter, Dana Louise Granby, born March 25, 1981. The meaning of life, motherhood, and womanhood was my daughter's gift to me as will be her gift from her child. These precious gifts of life and meaning inspire my intellectual concern that black families and black motherhood be dignified.

Intellectual support for this work flowed first from Dr. Jack Buerkle who encouraged me to pursue my interest in black families through sociological and then graduate study. Alan Kerckhoff, Richard Campbell, Larry Goodwin, Naomi Quinn, Carol Stack, Joel Smith, and Walter Allen all nurtured the earliest stages of this work.

Dr. Andrew Billingsley, President, Morgan State University, a great scholar, great institutional leader, and my mentor, fanned the flames of my enthusiasm for a just view of black families with the gifts of his tutelage and his love.

Without the kind and gracious assistance of Gloria Mims, Librarian, Special Collections, and Professor Lee Alexander, Archivist, Atlanta University Library, this work would not have been enriched by that great storehouse of black history. Phyllis Bischoff, Librarian, Special Collections, University of California, Berkeley, and Felix McKay, U.S. Census Bureau, were generous also in providing information that was needed for this research.

There were others, a legion of others, who by being and caring influenced my thoughts. Although unnamed, their influence is expressed in these pages.

Financial support for this work flowed in part from a University of California, Berkeley, faculty fellowship, from the Resource Center for Community Institutions, Oakland, California, and from Scientific and Management Research Group, San Jose, California, my business. Without Elaine Ridley, Secretary to the Resource Center, and Kelly M. Miller, the temporary typist who was literally "godsent," this manuscript would still be in draft.

Finally, this work manifests the unique contribution to my life and thought of a great man, a great community leader and humanist, Evelio Grillo. He is written into every line.

SCIENCE,
MYTH,
REALITY

1

Introduction

If there is one area of social life whose influence has touched almost every human being at some time, that area is the family. As the guardian of human survival, the family is entrusted with the nurturance of the neonate, the infant, the child, and the adult, and in doing that people undertake our differentiation from the rest of the animal kingdom. We have each survived and attained human status and so each of us has been loved and enveloped in some family experience. Though, in substance, such experiences may differ in certain specific ways from each other and be unique, in essence, there is something in the core of the family experience that transcends idiosyncracy, something universal that integrates the individual with nature and with the rest of humanity.

On the one hand, it could be argued that it is these qualities of universality and intimacy in the family experience that have advanced the field of family studies. That is, our own ties to our own families stimulate our interest in deriving family principles to be used in successive, successful generations. Our own family experience provides the empirical grounding for our theories and for hypotheses we desire to test. On the other hand, contingent upon perspective, it could also be argued that it is these qualities that have slowed the field and maintained its conservative tone. That is, our intimate ties to our families have confirmed our ethnocentric biases—made our experiences seem best of all. Our own family ties have fostered our exclusion of the tenability of other families and have constrained our definitions of the sources of our nature and nurture. In the same fashion we have constrained the nurturing and orienting family experience to a narrow span of life. Yet there is sufficient evidence that our character, appearance, temperament, and manner continually evolve as we love and are loved and as we nurture and are nurtured throughout our lives and away from those milieux into which we fall through accident of birth.

To some extent, it is fair to argue that students of the family have tended to view the phenomenon from either one or the other of these perspectives. Specifically, there has been a tendency to view the family as either moving onward and upward toward higher states or as declining, its downfall mirroring the evils of modern society and the triumph of nature over nurture. Many social scientists have attempted to describe families generically, assigning those of their own membership to higher levels than others on evolutionary continua; others elect to view families in descending order, in which case families that depart radically from the conventional in modern society are stratified inversely with respect to developmental continua. In this latter case, the loss of tradition is thought to be the loss of stability, and the loss of organization is thought to be decadent and an augur of extinction.

The rise of family study can be seen as coincident with the rise of colonialism, since within such political frameworks students of the family were afforded firsthand data and the study of "primitive" familism flourished. The colonial period ushered hundreds of Western social anthropologists into the virgin world of Eastern families, where there were seemingly astonishing differences in the way individuals were integrated with their nature and their essence. To Westerners, who often equated nakedness with a state of preparedness for sexual intercourse and for whom sexual intercourse was not attended with natural abandon, the ungarbed denizens of the tropics seemed to be preoccupied with sex. Even so, such "primitives" provided fertile data for the exploration of sexuality and other topics that to "moderns" were still enshrouded in a sacred mystique colored by religious belief. Along with the mission of seeking colonial lands for the ravenous masses of Europe went the task of "civilizing" the natives in order to bring them into line with the Western value system. The belief in the sanctity of the Western family colored interpretations of non-Western families that were, by comparison, profane, backward, evidence of the evolution of social organisms, and evidence that documented the progress of the Western world.

The influence of Darwin's evolutionism still looms in the sociology of the family, especially as sociologists investigate groups that differ from mainstream society, although social Darwinism has succumbed to other perspectives. The black family, reflective of some biological and cultural difference, has as such been subject to this influence as much as any other family group under study. Consistent with the competing perspectives of social science, multiform propositions have been asserted as explanations of the roles, structures, and functions of black families in the United States. The primary purposes of this work are to assess the validity of the most salient propositions in the field of family study regarding the Afro-American family in the United States; to examine the relationship of the propositions to emerging perspectives in the field; and to assess the quality of the research that the propositions have generated. Only by doing this assessment of the research does one get a sense of what is really known about black families.

A NOTE ON SCIENTIFIC METHOD AND REALITY

It is impossible to do, know, or understand everything sufficiently in modern society and, consequently, increasing reliance is placed on experts and technicians. A legislator or policymaker's vital concern with a social phenomenon must often be quickly translated into factual data and information, and the experts and technicians enlisted for this work are very often social scientists. The role of the enlisted scientist may be to share his/her knowledge, to examine the body of existing knowledge, or to produce some knowledge. In any case, what the legislator or policymaker learns about the topic will be a function of the work of the expert. The reality upon which the policymaker or legislator acts is a secondhand one, but one made credible by a high and respected source—the scientist.

Scientific reality, as we all know it, is the end result of a set of rules (deemed scientific) being applied to our attempts to gain knowledge about a phenomenon. The set of rules comprises the method and, it is argued, the more rigorously the rules are applied, the closer scientific reality approximates truth. In social science, particularly, the rigorous application of method, while idealized, is almost by definition rarely realized. The subject and data of social research—people—are rarely as calibrated as are other fine instruments, rarely as synchronized as fine "Swiss movement," and rarely of stable or static consistency. Consequently, social reality is often shifting, often negotiable, often untimely, often inarticulate. That something other than truth is often devised to influence social policy is no wonder; however, we should remain challenged to correct the distortions so created. The social scientist has a delicate and entrusted role in being the purveyor of reality to those who control the forces that shape it. Therefore, it is of grave concern that the social scientist make every attempt to align reality with truth through scrupulous scientific method.

2

Black Families and Family Theory: The Procrustean Bed

Major family theorists concede that in this century's quest to establish general family principles, efforts have as yet yielded only conceptual frameworks, which provide useful models for organizing the empirical world of families. Hill and Hansen, for example, identify five conceptual frameworks utilized in family study, some of these used more in earlier work on the family than in later ones.[1] Most of the frameworks so examined were conceptualized in response to the empirical stimuli of Western and mainstream American families. Often the analysis of ethnic and lower-class families within the context of these frameworks has, therefore, required truncation or stretching of data to fit the theoretical realities posed by them. Following is a discussion of these major theoretical frameworks, with some analysis of the perspectives they have brought to bear on black family research.[2]

THE INSTITUTIONAL FRAMEWORK

Utilizing the organismic analogy attributed to Herbert Spencer, a social Darwinist, students concerned with the historical development of the family, likened its development to that of an organ within an organismic whole—the society.[3] The family institution, when viewed on a historical continuum, is observed as having evolved through hierarchical, orderly stages of development. In relationship to their society, earlier families are thought to be different from later families in terms of their form and function, and families are generally described as ranging from lesser developed to more wholly developed family systems. Thus, preindustrial families, while not only being historically precedent to industrial families, were also viewed as being at less developed stages of progress. The greatest legacy of institutional analysis has been in historical and comparative studies, although the institutional focus precludes a concern with family internal dynamics or with specific family patterns.[4] Without knowledge of family internal dynamics, however, we do not know what families do, what holds them together, what breaks them apart. Without knowledge of family patterns, we do not know whether all families are the same, if they function the same, or how family patterns relate to family processes.

Early students in the institutional tradition who subscribed to theories of lineal evolution viewed the family as having evolved from some inchoate form, through polygamy to monogamy. Consequently, groups with monogamous families were thought to be more advanced than polygamous groups, and some believed non-Western societies to comprise populations of dubious evolutionary advance. While theories of lineal evolution are now generally discredited, contemporary institutionalists still find it useful to categorize complex time units of cultural change into periods of social evolution. Flowing from this tradition, are the typologies of societal types, based on organizational features, which are familiar to most social scientists, including agricultural/industrial and gemeinschaft/gesellschaft. These typologies are similar to Durkheim's classifications of cultural solidarity as mechanical and organic types, which are suggestive of *degrees* of simplicity. The untrained mind tends to focus on the extremes of these posited continua, however, and to dichotomize social reality. Such typologies aid the social scientist in theorizing about the correlates of family structure,[5] but in utilizing these types to do family research, the scientist may minimize the variance that really exists within society. The descriptive value of an operational approach would be illustrated in the hypotheses generated by the researcher's perspective. For example, village, tribal, urban, and national, community organizations were proposed to have differing effects on family organization—an intriguing hypothesis—since families in one social arena seemed ostensibly to differ from those in another. It was under such a theoretical influence that the first popular studies of black families in the United States appeared.

THE INSTITUTIONAL APPROACH TO THE BLACK FAMILY

Students of the "Chicago School" and the protégés of Robert E. Park and Ernest W. Burgess, Charles Spurgeon Johnson and E. Franklin Frazier are posited to have viewed the black family through the eyes of their mentors who in turn were firmly positioned in Spencerian thought. Robert E. Park, for example, had two parallel and overriding intellectual concerns—urbanization and race relations. His views that urbanization (1) embodies the process basic to civilization's evolution, (2) precedes more extensive social change, (3) provides a laboratory condition for the study of the variability in human nature, and (4) represents a causal nexus in the generation of social problems and social disorganization are all reflected in the focal concerns of his students, Johnson and Frazier.[6]

Johnson's study of six hundred families in Macon County, Alabama, focused on the correlates of what he termed "folk culture."[7] Folk culture differed from other forms in that those immersed in it were close to the land, had little resource beyond subsistence, and wrought most of their existence—their clothing, their furniture, their food—by hand: theirs was, literally, life "from scratch." Laboring under the influence of the Chicago School, Johnson reflected the views of his mentors toward the prevalence of illegitimacy, extended families, and other issues; that is, he saw these matters as manifestations of "the Negro problem," and his views have often been interpreted in that manner. Unlike his mentors, Johnson had a love and empathy for the folk of Macon County, which is often not captured in his published work. He writes very sensitively of illegitimacy, saying, for example, that it is often a consequence of later-than-average marriage, and "the postponement of marriage which is largely an economic necessity gives a different value to courtship. One result of this is a group rationalization as a substitute for early marriage as a control at this active sex period."[8] Sex experimentation, he argues, is natural and normal. Intimacy is taken for granted, and "an incidental value of this lack of a censoring public opinion is the freedom of children thus born from warping social condemnation."[9] What is more, Dr. Johnson clearly implicates the brutal tenant farming system as being the source of problems to the black families he studied, and it is clear from his early work that there is a distinction between the "Negro problem" and the "problems Negroes had." Charles S. Johnson and E. Franklin Frazier were concerned with the latter.

Although his empirical work was chiefly with black peasants, Johnson incorporates black family progress and variability theoretically with his notion of "cultural planes."[10] These, he argued, account for the often seeming inconsistencies in the status of blacks, that is, the upwardly mobile *slant*. Those who must share resources with impoverished relatives do not go up in a perpendicular fashion as their economic status is intimately linked and intertwined with the status of the folk back home. Those who are not so encumbered move up more quickly.

Frazier's use of the institutional framework was in his analysis of the impact of urbanization on the black family. He also was concerned with the "problems Negroes had," although he has often been interpreted as being a proponent of the "Negro problem" thesis. Frazier's overriding concern was in understanding the impact of urbanization on a largely agrarian people.[11] From this focus he examined the role of the three-generation head of household, the disruptive influence of migration on potentially stable unions, and the rising rates of social pathology associated with the crisis of migration.[12] Frazier, unlike his interpreters including Moynihan,[13] but like Johnson, charted the progress and development of black families by examining them in social, geographical, and historical contexts. Frazier and Johnson sought cures rather than causes for the problems. In contrast to the work of his mentors, Frazier's work examined the paths black men and women followed to urbanization. He examined the cultural patterns of the stable upper and middle classes[14] as well as those of the peasant and urbanizing classes.[15]

And nowhere in his work does he *not* express optimism for the alleviation of the problems blacks have, given economic opportunity. It is in this area in which Frazier has been most misread, since his seminal work on black families[16] was extensively used in support of the cyclical theory of black pathology posited by the U.S. Department of Labor in the form of the Moynihan report.[17]

A NOTE ON VALUES IN WRITING, EDITING, AND READING

There have been mixed criticisms leveled toward the early institutional analyses of black family life and culture. Most of this criticism has been in response to the published work. Frazier, especially, has been lambasted for his popularization of the concept of "matriarchy,"[18] but only after the concept was employed by his interpreters with quite a different tone. In rereading Frazier in attempts to redeem him from the work of the U.S. Department of Labor,[19] I have found between the lines, as in Johnson's writings, love, compassion, comfort, and the search for understanding of the agony in the human condition. This finding is quite different from that in the work of those who seek a scapegoat for the evils of the economic system. How different is the role of the matriarch described by Frazier:

> A large proportion of each generation of Negro mothers in these rural areas continue to bear patiently the burden of motherhood and assume responsibility for the support of their children. Their daughters still follow in their footsteps and bring their offspring to the maternal household. Then these mothers are elevated to the dignity of grandmothers, a position which gives them a peculiar authority in family relations and places on them the responsibility for keeping the kindred together.[20]

Or Johnson:

> Again, there are the competent, self-sufficient women who not only desire children but need them as later aids in the struggle for survival

when their strength begins to wane. They want neither the restriction of a formal marriage contract, nor the association with a husband. They get children, not so much through weakness as through their own deliberated selection of a father.[21]

In the process from conceptualization to widely disseminated publication of ideas are the same pitfalls to human understanding as there are in other areas of human relations. Why are the love and compassion of Johnson and Frazier for the people they studied not obvious in their published works? My reading of unpublished and primary work suggests that the editorial process to which their work was submitted was one in which ideas in conflict with those popular at the time were expurgated from the context. This, of course, speaks to the values in reading and editing and suggests that the institutions which are media for reality must also be committed to dissemination of those realities that approximate truth. Perhaps one of the factors which has affected the quality of research in the institutional perspective is the historical focus of institutional analyses. Few data are available for rigorously controlled historical analyses. However, many of the propositions developed by institutional theorists have been explored within the context of theoretical frameworks, which are more amenable to empirical research, and they are being tested more carefully as theories and methods evolve toward complexity.

THE STRUCTURAL-FUNCTIONAL FRAMEWORK

The family is a subsystem of interlocking roles that closely interacts with other subsystems or institutions, the total of which make up society.[22] The family, as a subsystem of society, functions to perpetuate itself and to maintain the larger social system of which it is a part. By focusing on the structural principles of the family, students of this persuasion attempt to discern the import of these principles for social relationships. The structural perspective becomes more complex than the institutional framework as it incorporates the interplay of the family subsystem with other institutions in society.

The structural-functional perspective has been often criticized because within it the individual is generally viewed less as an active initiator of social events and more as a reactor to structural influences. It is also maintained that the structural-functional approach takes a static view of the family, capturing its structural features at one point in time and relating them to other institutional arrangements.[23] As a result, it is argued, actual variance in familial structures and functions is neglected.

As in the bio-physical sciences, there is a tendency among structural-functional sociologists to view the predetermined structure of an organism as being in its "best" state. Therefore, rigid adherents to this perspective have tended to view deviant structures as malfunctioning if not non-functional. This perspective does not segment a society into subgroups with differing structures for positive functioning; from this perspective, therefore, black families have been made to appear very deviant. Social anthropologists have made heavy contributions within this framework. The institutional features upon which they have focused are family composition, residence rules, kinship rules and obligations, parental and conjugal authority patterns, marriage forms and rules, and the structural consequences of these features for society as a whole. When structural-functional research is done with non-Western groups, evaluative questions do not arise since, whatever the society's modal pattern, it is usually considered the "best" state for that particular society.

STRUCTURAL-FUNCTIONAL APPROACHES TO THE BLACK FAMILY

While the structural-functional perspective might prove useful to investigators of the modal American family system, the foci of this perspective (family composition and residence and kinship, for example) assume the roles for these to be the same among American subgroups and thus predefine the black U.S. family as deviant in structure and therefore malfunctional. To some extent it is the underlying assumption of systemic homeostasis or "best state" which has made it a poor perspective for the study of black families. Such an assumption is based on the belief that black families have been influenced only by cultural forces indistinguishable from those that influence white families.[24] Therefore, a popular belief is that they have operated consistent with a modal American world view and are subject to the impact of the same ecological forces. Despite the considerable research that contradicts this model of reality with evidence of at least a synthetic culture among American subgroups, many of the prominent propositions regarding the black family are not yet informed by the new theoretical frameworks.

The U.S. Department of Labor publication, basing much of its analysis on Daniel P. Moynihan's interpretation of Frazier,[25] argues that urbanization had a disorganizing effect on black family structure through a selection process wherein the female-headed household was successful during slavery and continued to thrive. Factors in the urban environment that caused the continued selection of this household type, according to the argument, are the mass recruitment of women into the labor force and the greater ease with which women can procure welfare services—both of these being factors which free women from the instrumental control of males. Since the instrumental male role is culturally valued, the ineffectiveness of the black male in this sphere, the Department of Labor argues, relegates him to further subordinancy vis-à-vis his partner; often his recourse is desertion, separation, or divorce—factors which further influence the incidence of female-headed households.[26]

In essence, the argument posited by this report is a sexist one in which the female partner is placed in the position of being either economically dependent or the cause of marital discord. In fact, the implicit argument is that male control over females is necessary and, without it, women should be left to head their own families.[27]

The argument continues: deprived of fulfillment of male instrumental roles, the black male enters into casual relationships with black females. Relationships are largely expressive and based on sexual interaction. Such relationships, the report argues, do not lead to concern for the women or any offspring of such unions. Because the valued role for men is instrumental, and the black male's capacity to establish an instrumental basis for interaction is a tenuous one, black male-female interaction is interpreted as exploitative and, further, the report posits, exploitation is evidenced in high rates of illegitimacy, unacknowledged paternity, and amarital sexual interaction. Because the culturally designated arena for sexual activity is within the matrimonially sanctioned conjugal group, the perspective brought to bear on sexual interaction among black people has been one that views such interaction as deviant and as a contributor to the presumed disorganization of the black community.

A pathological male role has been argued to have become culturally stabilized so that even within isolated nuclear black family units, the male is theorized to be remiss in those instrumental, superordinate qualities that are necessary to the equilibrium of the family system. Like most machines in disequilibrium, the argument goes, the black family has fallen short of fulfilling its functions. Thus faulty socialization produces delinquency, mental malfunctionaries, low educational attainment, and all of the inadequacies that flow from them, according to this Department of Labor report. Faulty performance of instrumental tasks, it argues, produces poverty and high welfare utilization. As the modal American family has been posited to have evolved from a total institution, to an interactional system whose primary function is that of providing emotional gratification for its members, so the black family system, the labor department study maintains, leaves its members emotionally starved. Thus, marriage is devalued by the unmarried and unfulfilling to the married—arguments which herald a dying system, a mechanical breakdown—implying an interventionary remedy that would be directed at black families themselves, rather than at the societal forces with which they interact.[28]

Consistent with these criticisms of the structural-functional perspective is the fact that where empirical studies have been undertaken to develop theory, investigators have tended to focus on highly urbanized, ghettoized, and impoverished segments of the black population, in effect, biasing their probabilities of observing pathology. The net result, of course, has been a distorted picture that proffers the lifestyle of a minority as the modal black family system.

Systemic models of family structures and functions ignore the internal dynamics of families—the dynamics through which societal values are transmitted and through which individual family members become socialized to family and societal culture. Without analysis of family interaction and its outcomes, there is no empirical basis for the propositions defining black family life.

THE INTERACTIONAL FRAMEWORK

The interactional framework following Burgess's definition of the family as a "unit of interacting personalities," provides a model for examining the overt interactions of family members.[29] The "family interactionists' " contention is that each person in the family unit occupies a position to which normatively prescribed roles are assigned and bases his/her behavior on perceived expectations regarding those roles. Interaction initiated by one family member is interpreted by another whose subjective definition of the objective situation will influence his/her behavior and, therefore, future interactional sequences. The interactionists argue that because there are "ego-needs" or emotional satisfactions derived from interaction with other persons, the family becomes the primary arena in which self-conceptions are built and personalities are formed, especially as desired characteristics are molded and shaped through ego rewards.

The interactional sequence is viewed as a critical variable determining the extent of conflict or harmony, or both moods, within the family. From an incipient gesture to the ego, the ego will define the situation and receive a "self-image" which may or may not be consistent with his/her self-concept. If the image the ego gets in such an interaction is one to which he/she assigns less positive value than to his/her self-concept, then the response gesture is likely to be one designed to promote the ego. Alternatively, if the image the ego gets is satisfactory, interaction is likely to proceed without conscious attention to ego needs. It is in such interactional sequences, according to the interactionists, that family members may construct a network of role expectations and a repertoire of expectations of each other that make family life orderly and predictable.[30] It is through this construction process that the family functions to socialize future members of society into acceptable roles and adult personalities of society become stabilized.[31]

The focus of the interactionists' framework on the internal dynamics of the family ignores the effects that forces external to the family have on the members and, consequently, we do not observe the link between structural forces and family interaction processes. While this perspective should, ideally, be useful in discerning the factors that intervene between social structural forces and behavioral outcomes, most research done on interaction in families is not so encompassing. Instead, researchers generally accept social structural theory as accurate and proceed to study family dynamic processes, such as decisionmaking, authority patterns, status relations, and communication. Although this has not been a widely used perspective for the study of black family behavior, the acceptance of these guiding theories has meant acceptance of the pathological perspective of black families. Thus, when interactionist researchers have concerned themselves with black families, they have focused upon discerning the interactional correlates of the deviance which they already assume to exist.

THE INTERACTIONAL APPROACH TO
THE BLACK FAMILY

Perusal of the limited research on the black family done from an interactionist's perspective reveals a startling attention to black dating and sexual patterns and a shocking inattention to "family" interactional patterns. To some extent, it might be fair to say that this is a function of existing data sources, that is, information is largely gained from captive audiences of high school and college students. The study of family interaction requires a much more voluntary group and more intimate interaction in the research process. Often such information must be gained from family counseling agencies and service agencies, and these may not be as heavily utilized by black as by white families.

More than being a theory for guiding research on black families, the interactional perspective has been a framework for interpreting findings. Its heavy emphasis on psychological tradition and concepts that have no empirical referents has provided license for the less scrupulous researcher to enter into speculative and often ungrounded debate about the moral status of black family members and has represented a "declaration of open season" for "radical empiricists" and "armchair theorists" with interest in making a statement about some presumed differences in black family and socialization processes.

Borrowing Freudian and neo-Freudian psychological theories, situational and structural-functional theorists' preclusions of black family malfunctionality, and the position-role-status paradigm of the interactionist scientific perspective, social scientists have documented black male adolescents into the "damned-if-you-do, damned-if-you-don't" position of being at once lacking in masculine identification and, at the same time, "defensively" masculine. This fact alone stands as evidence of the lack of conceptual and, therefore, theoretical clarity in the field.[32]

Propositions concerning interactional relationships in the black family can be classified as (1) those concerning premarital interaction, (2) those concerning marital interaction, and (3) those concerning parent-child interaction.

In the black premarital dyad, it is proposed the male and female motives are variant, with the objective of the male being sex, and the objective of the female, marriage.

Such a state is argued to generate exploitative relationships since the bargaining power of females is considerably lessened by a shortage of males. Blacks are proposed to be more sexually permissive (with a negative connotation), and this is argued to be reflected in the higher rates of premarital coitus and pregnancy of blacks than whites. Sexual activity is argued to be less gratifying due to exploitation.[33] Not only does such a position assume some accuracy in rates of reported premarital sex and pregnancy, but it also assumes that: (1) females desire sex only conditionally, that is, with marriage, (2) female sex is a commodity with which she bargains, and (3) sex is only gratifying if she is able to successfully manipulate with it. The same view of reality is carried into models where investigators of the black conjugal dyad argue that women no longer bargain for marriage but for instrumental rewards that men bring to the union. This situation is posited to create particularly tenuous relationships in black dyads, especially as black men are often subject to unemployment and discrimination in employment.[34] Interactionists further argue that the salience of black females in instrumental activities undermines the role of the spouse, lessens his bargaining power, makes him uncertain as to his authority and creates his withdrawal from decision-making processes—the major tasks around which families are organized and the bases for marital bonding.[35] Such deviant role performance, it is argued, leads to mutual dissatisfaction with the marital bond and results in higher rates of marital instability.[36]

The deviant role perspective is also brought to bear on the study of black socialization processes. The black female's salience in instrumental activities is proposed to cause her neglect of her socialization and expressive functions, which then prematurely forces her child to rely on peers for socialization and for emotional gratification.[37] The absence of maternal control and supervision then is posited to be a primary causal factor of high rates of delinquency, illegitimacy, educational dropouts, and so on. While there has been no research in which black maternal employment has been empirically directly related to child-rearing practices, propositions have been generated simply on the basis of studies that have shown differences in child-rearing practices for blacks and whites. The most often cited study of black/white child rearing shows blacks to be permissive in areas of toilet training.[38] The attribution of pathological outcomes to these differences, however, is usually done on a post hoc basis by other investigators, as the original researchers have neither established nor even suggested such a relationship.

The same theoretical posture is maintained with respect to the female-headed family, more of which occur among blacks.

The absent black male is posited to be a prime factor in the sex role deviance of male adolescents, leaving them without models for identification, which is purported to be evidenced in low aspirations toward traditional roles. This and the identification of black females with the "dominant" female role are argued to be the outcomes of faulty socialization processes—the malfunctioning black family's inability to place its children in socially required roles.[39]

To summarize, interactionist theorists have argued (without regard to social-structural influences) that: (1) sex role deviance is a feature of the black conjugal dyad; (2) as a consequence, deviant role identification is a feature in the socialization of its offspring; and (3) as a further consequence, the black adolescent faces the adult environment grossly unprepared to function in the dominant cultural milieu wherein men and women engage in sexual bargaining with *his* instrumental rewards and *her* expressive rewards.

THE SITUATIONAL FRAMEWORK

The situational framework defines the family as a situation that impinges itself on the personality and behavior of its members. From this perspective, the family is classified as being a situational type along certain dimensions—for example, structural, processual, or dealing with content—and studied as an independent variable effecting personality and behavioral responses.[40]

Situational researchers have studied "the lower-class home," "the overindulgent home," and other areas in family culture. Except as being black is defined as a condition itself, the black family has not been studied from the situational perspective.

THE DEVELOPMENTAL FRAMEWORK

A relatively recent approach, the developmental perspective, has the potential for integrating the institutional, structural-functional, and interactional approaches. Borrowing concepts from these approaches, this framework permits the study of changes in family roles as they are influenced by forces both external and internal to family units.[41] At the same time, the developmental framework incorporates variations generated by changes in family composition. Seen from this perspective, the family has certain developmental tasks relative to its age, sex, and other compositional features, which make it similar to other families of the same demographic makeup, but also unlike those of other composition. The developmental perspective affords, therefore, a useful classification device for family study and, at the same time, enables elucidation of the variance that might be hidden by other approaches.

From the developmental perspective, families' internal and external influences can be studied first within the context of conjugal pairs, later as families of procreation, with the addition of offspring, later as families with school-aged children, then with adolescents, later after the children are launched as adults, and finally in senior status and old age.

Since researchers have tended to minimize the actual variance among black families for the sake of generalization, they have not used the developmental approach. Their tendencies have been instead to focus on families in their childbearing years, and most propositions deal with the theme of functionality, which heavily relies on familial or societal reproduction. Almost nothing is known of preprocreant black families, of middle-aged black families, of those parenting young adults, or of those whose children have become adults. Although high rates of remarriage exist, there is nothing known about "stepparenting" black families. There has been some recent attention to the black aged, generated by modern interests in social gerontology.

PHENOMENOLOGICAL APPROACHES TO THE BLACK FAMILY

While most discussions of family theories and frameworks do not differentiate the anthropological approach from the structural-functional approach, there is developing a notable difference in much of the anthropological literature.[42] Many ethnographers have begun to inject an approach into the study of the black family, which may be termed *phenomenological*, chiefly because it is an attempt to get at the point of view of black families. Such a perspective has introduced a body of literature concerning black families that appears to be either more "value free" or "value explicit." There is nothing so pure as "value free" social science, but the literature to which I refer does not apply white middle-class values to the analysis of other groups. Many concepts used by anthropologists do not symbolize, a priori, devaluation of that which is different. This has been much of the problem with the research on black families. While anthropologists generally adopt a functional framework, the rise of the field in the study of non-Western culture saw its need for value-free concepts to describe culturally patterned behavior. When behaviors deviant from Western patterns are discerned by anthropologists, they are viewed as functional for the requirements of that particular society. As a result, a lexicon of descriptive terms is employed that does not reflect the ideals of Western society.

While it has been an American sociological tradition to view blacks as culturally stripped,[43] many anthropologists have rejected this position.[44] When the anthropological framework is carried over to the phenomenological study of black communities, the communities are viewed as tenable cultural structures that embody world views and ideologies for survival, just as other societies do. Consequently, the assumption of malfunctionality held by sociologists is replaced by assumptions of functionality, and the investigators seek explanations as to why certain behaviors are functional and how they become patterned to maintain the particular social system. The researcher then looks for stability, rather than instability.

Concepts such as kin, quasi kin, and friend acknowledge the potential scope of socializing black family agents. Often, however, researchers regard only the isolated black nuclear unit as valid for socialization functions and predefine as malfunctional the extended unit.[45]

Whereas the term *fosterage* is used by anthropologists to describe a tradition of grandmothers assuming major responsibilities for child rearing,[46] the same tradition has been described by others as "grandmothers' greed for babies."[47] Anthropologists, who do not hold the assumption that fathers must occupy the same household as mothers and children, have located fathers and paternal influences which other researchers preclude themselves from locating.[48] By focusing on social networks, rather than on isolated units, phenomenological and anthropological researchers have located groupings which fulfill functions that other researchers have argued only the nuclear family is capable of fulfilling.[49]

The propositions synthesized from the body of phenomenological literature produced mostly by anthropologists and regarding black families follow.

1. Obligatory kin and friendship ties that are based on exchange, cooperation, and caring are activated in communities where members have low economic standing.[50]
2. The inaccessibility of public goods and services to males makes females salient in the relationships of these families to public agencies. Those who assume male/female relationships to have an economic core, have interpreted such an imperative for survival as a sign of female dominance which effects male alienation from the family.[51]
3. In contrast to this position, phenomenological researchers have noted a moving to the periphery of economic activities by males who may remain at the center of familial relationships.[52]
4. It is possible, therefore, for males to be loving, clandestine, and dominant forces.[53]
5. While public imperatives may require male absence, the male's actual role may be that of a socially acceptable mate to a woman and a father to his and/or her children who interacts with them on a regular basis.[54]
6. The male may be listed in the census of a kin-based household different from the one in which his mate is listed.[55]

7. Surrounding this pair and their offspring may be a web of kin and nonkin personalities with whom they are all obligated to exchange, cooperate, and seek survival.[56]

8. As an adaptive strategy, this perspective argues, the survival of an extended social network becomes more highly valued than the survival of an isolated nuclear unit.[57]

9. Given the tenuous ability of black males to remain economically stable over long periods of time, in this milieu forces militate against the formation of these units.[58]

10. Their probable destinies will be disintegration and re-integration of their constituents into a stronger network which may be extended.[59]

11. This perspective argues that it is not matriarchal women who militate against the existence of the isolated units valued by the dominant society, but, instead, it is the tenability of the extended network over the isolated unit for survival of depressed communities.[60]

REWRITING BLACK FAMILY THEORY

There are several sources of support for the rewriting of history and, therefore, for the rewriting of black family theory. Within the past decade there have been at least two major intellectual developments which have advanced the field: 1) empirically based historical revisions which posit slave creative culture and 2) the taking seriously of Eastern philosophies and correlative attempts to measure the influence of African-based philosophical systems on African-Americans.

Whereas the tradition has been to view black families as being either "made in America" by the structural forces of slavery, racism, and continued discrimination, or, at best, mimetically pursuing the dreams of acceptance and achievement, the evidence for these views has been slight. Historians have considered evidence that slaves, although they came from many different tribes in Africa, had more commonalities than differences.

The philosophical systems and world views that grew from their interaction with the African topography and ecology evoked similar responses to their antebellum condition.[61] A slave culture was synthesized from the African past and the American reality of the antebellum period.[62]

Nobles notes in his analysis of African philosophical systems that there are elements in the African world view that facilitated the survival of black slave communities and contemporary Afro-American communities.[63] Specifically, he cites the view of the world in which there is consciousness of oneness of being, and interdependence. The unit of existence, he posits, is greater than one—it is family. Such a view still prevails in varying degrees in Afro-American families.[64]

To some extent the infamous debate between Melville Herskovits,[65] who saw Africanisms in Afro-American culture and E. Franklin Frazier,[66] whose intellectual orientation was toward assimilation and saw none, has been revived and, perhaps, resolved.

The emergent popularity of oral history techniques[67] as a method of linking the present to the past, the wide availability of slave narrative data, and the emergence of black scholars who apply different perspectives to old data have all facilitated recent developments in theory.

Herbert Gutman, a labor historian, examined a plantation birth register covering the period 1760 to 1857.[68] The particular plantation he studied recorded the names of slave fathers as well as mothers, so that Gutman was able to elaborate a kinship system and chart. Among other things, the following flowed from his analysis.

1. A bilateral kinship system was maintained by the slaves through given names.
2. Given names linked offspring to larger kin networks and especially to fathers.
3. There were peculiarly Afro-American domestic rules, organization, and networks that were maintained by slave beliefs and values.

4. Cultural taboos forced exogamy among the slaves, so that while "cousin-marriage" predominated in slave-holding and white society, it apparently did not exist among the slaves.[69]

The evidence for slave creative culture has been well documented, however efforts to disseminate these new findings have not been sufficient to eliminate the stereotypes that were supported by less rigorous science.

Among the African cultural continuities noted by Nobles in modern black families, in metropolitan San Francisco, were family networking, between consanguineal (blood-related) families, conjugal (marriage-related) families, and interactional or fictive families; and structural elasticity in the families such that families often accommodated new members, whether blood or nonblood.

These families and networks provide each other with child care, counseling, financial aid, and other supports that often fall in the domain of family and institutional support. Nobles noted, also, that families were characterized by flexibility in role performance, although role definitions conformed to standard concepts of masculinity and femininity. He, therefore, states that ". . . the black family is thought an 'Americanized African family.' It is African in nature and American in nurture (training). The observable behavioral outcomes, therefore, must be interpreted in terms of understanding the American conditions which influence their development and/or expression."[70]

While it is true that some black families are completely Anglicized and Americanized, it is also true that there are many who find their support, sustenance, and survival in their traditions. Often these are southern, rural, and the legacy of slave and African cultures. A number of black persons are flexible in their enactment of cultural roles and shift back and forth as deemed necessary, exhibiting varying degrees of "blackness."[71] This role flexibility and adaptability has been functional to black survival.[72]

The failure of social science to see African continuities in the Afro-American experience is symptomatic of several problems.

1. There has been a tendency of Western social science to seek linear explanations of nonlinear phenomena. Explanations tend to be additive. Therefore things are expected to be either one thing or another. Men and women are expected to be instrumental *or* expressive; therefore, when black women worked they were called the matriarchs—the power and authority—in black families, and black men were described as feminine in identity and ineffectual as males.[73] Women were assigned to the house, and men to the labor force.

   Frazier and Herskovits reached an impasse since blacks had to be either African or American. When reality gets dichotomized in this fashion and calls attention to extremes and polar concepts, it is difficult to see interactions or the simultaneous occurrence of events. Consequently we do not understand or incorporate women with concepts of themselves as providers and men with concepts of themselves as nurturant. These characteristics among blacks flow directly from the African experience and from its interaction with the brutality of chattel slavery and racial discrimination and hostility.

2. The perspective of the non-Western world has been virtually ignored by Western social science. American scholars have focused primarily on the European experience, and consequently books on world history have included African history only as it relates to Africa as part of European colonial history.

3. Western social scientists have been, for the most part, conceptually bankrupt when it comes to even the possibility of observing, describing, and understanding black-American culture.

4. Black families often have been put on the defensive about "who they are." Stigma associated with blackness, media portrayal of Africans, the reward for "white ways" and features, all gave little incentive for accepting, let alone being proud of and asserting, one's Africanness.

These emerging theoretical perspectives hold promise for present and future research. Black families and black social scientists have yet to develop a self-created, self-critical, framework of analysis for the understanding of black families. It is clear that in being self-critical we blacks must acknowledge the duality of our essence, even as did W. E. B. Du Bois, a great scholar who was one of the earliest students of the black family.

> The history of the American Negro is the history of this strife—this longing to attain self-conscious manhood, to merge his double self into a better and truer self. In this merging he wishes neither of the older selves to be lost. He would not bleach his Negro soul in a flood of white Americanism, for he knows that Negro blood has a message for the world. He simply wishes to make it possible for a man to be both a Negro and an American.[74]

THEORETICAL OVERVIEW

Overwhelmingly, the perspectives brought to bear on the study of the black family have been generated by the institutional, structural-functional, and interactional frameworks of analysis. While one's first impression might be that the conclusions regarding the black family generated by these three frameworks complement one another, a perusal of the literature makes one excruciatingly aware of the gap between theory and research and sensitive to the role of values, assumptions, and the philosophical underpinnings of the researcher.

The institutional framework relies heavily on evolutionary theory and "documents" historically the necessary transition from slavery of the black family institution under "civilizing" influences. The structural-functional framework picks up this theme in making analogies between the isolated nuclear family and an organism in homeostasis or a machine in equilibrium. The assumptions regarding role requirements for equilibrium predefine the malfunctioning of black families that do not manifest these roles and, as such, provide a theme to be picked up by interactionist researchers who then have ignored external influences.

There has as yet been no systematic research that begins with the social-structural placement of black families at each stage of the family life cycle and relates this placement first to belief systems and, finally, to the adult social placement of its offspring in occupational worlds and in other families of procreation. Yet, there is much literature that contains such global descriptions of black families. I contend, however, that because of the divorce between theory and research, such descriptions have been derived from speculation and from incorporating in the literature the out of context views generated from the many theoretical perspectives.

New models hold some promise for aiding our understanding of black families in that they incorporate the realities of Africanness, cultural dualism, and cultural change. Many propositions generated by the new theoretical perspectives can be tested, although they have not as yet been incorporated into established social scientific paradigms. Established social science is, of course, conservative and prefers neatly coded concepts, random samples, and quantitative data. Hypotheses generated in the new perspectives merit testing and can be tested within the guidelines of established and traditional social science. That is, samples can be collected on a random basis; sizeable samples can be generated; and many concepts can be quantified.

It is my contention that the cleavage between theory and hypothesis testing need not exist. It does, however, and represents a serious problem in the field of black family study. Whether the problem is an intellectual or methodological one, or a result of a less rational clinging to traditional values, is moot, since the results are the same. Observation, questions, even the choice of design require selection. Selection is an intellectual act, but it is an act that requires knowledge—that material that is valued and chosen from all that exists and that becomes culturally ordained as the intellectual wealth of a society.

Social scientists, for the most part, have selected models and methods that distort family realities. By distorting family realities to fit theories, social scientists have done little to advance families or family theory. Whatever families are, their primary role is a humanizing one—one in which we derive imperatives for our survival. The role of social science then should be to develop models for the survival of humanity. There is much to teach humanity about survival, which flows from the experience of black families.

NOTES

1. Reuben Hill and Donald A. Hansen, "The Identification of Conceptual Frameworks Utilized in Family Study." *Marriage and Family Living.* 22:299-311. 1960.

2. Procrustes, a figure in Greek mythology, was a robber whose victims' legs he either stretched—if too short—or amputated—if too long—to fit the iron bed on which he forced them to lie. "The Bed of Procrustes" has become proverbial for inflexibility and distortion.

3. See Lewis A. Coser and Bernard Rosenberg, *Sociological Theory: A Book of Readings.* New York: Macmillan. 1969; and Lewis A. Coser, *Masters of Sociological Thought.* New York: Harcourt Brace Jovanovich. 1971.

4. See John Sjirmaki, "The Institutional Approach." In Harold T. Christensen, ed., *Handbook of Marriage and the Family.* Chicago: Rand McNally. 1964.

5. Ibid.

6. Robert E. Park and Ernest W. Burgess, *Introduction to the Science of Sociology.* Chicago: University of Chicago Press. 1924.

7. Charles Spurgeon Johnson, *Shadow of the Plantation.* Chicago: University of Chicago Press. 1934.

8. Charles Spurgeon Johnson, Untitled. Atlanta University. Atlanta University Archives, Cullen-Jackman Memorial Manuscript Collection, Charles Spurgeon Johnson Papers, 1893-1956.

9. Ibid.

10. Johnson, *Shadow of the Plantation.*

11. E. Franklin Frazier, *The Negro Family in the United States.* Chicago: University of Chicago Press. 1939.

12. Ibid.

13. Moynihan, *The Negro Family.*

14. E. Franklin Frazier, *Black Bourgeoisie.* New York: Collier Books. 1957.

15. Frazier, *The Negro Family in the United States.*

16. Ibid.

17. Moynihan, *The Negro Family.*

18. Frazier, *The Negro Family in the United States.*

19. Moynihan, *The Negro Family.*

20. Frazier, *The Negro Family in the United States.* Page 133.

21. Johnson, Untitled.

22. See Talcott Parsons and Robert F. Bales, *Family, Socialization and Interaction Process.* New York: Free Press. 1955; and Christensen, *Handbook of Marriage and the Family.*

23. Ibid.

24. Wade W. Nobles, in describing the prevailing perspectives on black families says that viewing them as "culturally stripped" is to argue that they are "made in America." See *A Formulative and Empirical Study of Black Families.* U.S. Department of Health, Education and Welfare. 1976.

25. Moynihan, *The Negro Family;* and Frazier, *The Negro Family in the United States.*

26. Moynihan, *The Negro Family.*

27. See Moynihan, *The Negro Family.*

28. Ibid.

29. Ralph H. Turner, *Family Interaction.* New York: John Wiley & Sons. 1970.

30. Ibid.

31. See Talcott Parsons, *Family, Civilization.*

32. See, for example, Henry B. Biller, "A Note on Father Absence and Masculine Development in Lower Class Negro and White Boys." *Child Development.* 39(11):1003-1006. 1968.

33. Lee Rainwater, "Some Aspects of Lower-Class Sexual Behavior." *Journal of Social Issues.* 22:96-108. 1966.

34. Robert O. Blood and Donald M. Wolfe, *Husbands and Wives.* New York: Free Press. 1960.

35. Turner, *Family Interaction.*

36. Blood and Wolfe, *Husbands and Wives.*

37. Moynihan, *The Negro Family.*

38. Allison Davis and Robert J. Havighurst, "Social Class and Color Differences in Child Rearing." *American Sociological Review.* 11:698-710. 1946.

39. See Moynihan, *The Negro Family*; and Roger Harvey Rubin, *Matricentric Family Structure and the Self-Attitudes of Negro Children.* San Francisco: R & E Publishing Co. 1976.

40. See Christensen, *Handbook.*

41. Ibid.

42. See Joyce Aschenbrenner, *Lifelines: Black Families in Chicago.* New York: Holt, Rinehart and Winston. 1975; and Carol B. Stack, *All Our Kin: Strategies for Survival in a Black Community.* New York: Harper and Row. 1974.

43. See especially E. Franklin Frazier, *The Negro Family in the United States;* and Nathan Glazer and Daniel P. Moynihan, *Beyond the Melting Pot.* Second edition. Cambridge, Mass.: M.I.T. Press. 1970.

44. Melville J. Herskovits and a host of black scholars have always rejected this position and found evidence of an African heritage among black Americans. However, such a concept has not as yet been given credibility within established social science. See Melville J. Herskovits, *The Myth of the Negro Past.* Boston: Beacon Press. 1958.

45. See Stack, *All Our Kin.*

46. Ibid.

47. David A. Schulz, *Coming Up Black.* Englewood Cliffs, N.J.: Prentice-Hall. 1969.

48. See Beverly O. Ford, "Case Studies of Black Female Heads of Household in the Welfare System: Socialization and Survival." *Western Journal of Black Studies.* 1(2):114-118. 1977. Also see Elliot Liebow, *Tally's Corner.* Boston: Little Brown. 1967.

49. Stack, *All Our Kin.*

*50. Ibid.

51. Moynihan, *The Negro Family.*

52. Ford, *Case Studies;* Stack, *All Our Kin.*

53. Ford, *Case Studies.*

54. Lovelene Earl and Nancy Lohmann, "Absent Fathers and Black Male Children." *Social Work.* 23(5):413-415. 1978.

55. Stack, *All Our Kin.*

56. Aschenbrenner, *Lifelines;* Stack, *All Our Kin;* Liebow, *Tally's Corner.*

57. Stack, *All Our Kin.*

58. Ibid.

59. Ibid.

60. Ibid.

61. For a discussion of Africanisms in black American world view see Wade W. Nobles, "Toward an Empirical and Theoretical Framework for Defining Black Families." *Journal of Marriage and the Family.* 40(4):679-688. 1979.

62. See Herbert G. Gutman, *The Black Family in Slavery and Freedom, 1750-1925.* New York: Pantheon. 1976.

63. Wade W. Nobles, *A Formulative and Empirical Study of Black Families.* Final Report. U.S. Department of Health, Education and Welfare. 1976.

64. Ibid.

65. See Herskovits, *The Myth of the Negro Past.*

66. Frazier, *The Negro Family in the United States.*

67. See, for example, Theodore Rosengarten, *All God's Dangers: The Life of Nate Shaw.* New York: Avon. 1974.

68. Gutman, *The Black Family.*

69. Ibid.

70. Nobles, *Formulative and Empirical Study.* Page 148.

71. Alan Counter notes this ability, even to the extent of shifting levels of language spoken, among the descendants of black slaves who escaped Dutch traders in Surinam. Alan Counter, "In Search of the Bush Afro-American." Symposium. University of California, Berkeley. May 1977.

72. Several slave narratives describe slaves' enactment of various roles in order to shield or protect family members. See, for example, Gilbert Osofsky, ed., *Puttin' on Ole Massa.* New York: Harper & Row. 1969.

73. Blood and Wolfe in *Husbands and Wives* use this conceptual framework when studying power among black and white families. Yet African men, slave fathers, and contemporary Afro-American fathers have all been noted to be expressive and instrumental in their relationships to their wives and children. African women, slave women, and contemporary Afro-American women have always been instrumental and expressive in their family roles. See Jomo Kenyatta, *Facing Mount Kenya.* New York: Vintage. 1965; and John Blassingame, *The Slave Community.* New York: Oxford University Press. 1972.

74. W. E. B. Du Bois, *The Souls of Black Folk.* 1903. New York: Premier Edition. 1961. Page 17.

3

The Demographic Status of Black Families

The following analysis is based on census data, and because of my concerns and questions regarding the validity of the data, I advise reading cautiously.

Foremost among my concerns is the U.S. Bureau of the Census's definition of the family as "two or more persons living together and related by blood, marriage or adoption."[1] This definition does not encompass the existence of all families, and especially of black families. The black family is a cultural tradition which incorporates consanguinity, but does not exclude nonblood ties;[2] incorporates formal, legal marriage, but does not exclude other marital bonds;[3] and incorporates court adjudicated adoption, but does not make that a necessary condition for family ties where an individual needs a family but is not related by blood or marriage.[4]

Second, there is the practice, although less frequent, of lumping "other" races with blacks, without specification of who they are and without analysis of the degree to which they are analogous, in fact, in any dimension.[5]

Third, there is the practice of presenting data on black families as ratios to white family data and of comparing blacks to whites. These methods have served to establish white patterns as norms and black patterns as deviations.[6]

Census bureau analyses that lump ages "14-34" into the same category are of limited utility in understanding the factors that affect the families of the young.[7] It is likely that there are differences between families headed by fourteen year olds and those headed by thirty-four year olds.

The census bureau has tended to view households as coterminous with families and household heads as family heads. This practice is frequently not the case with black families.

In many reports, the census bureau has included the households headed by men who are in the military and men who are incarcerated with those headed by women.[8] Given the disproportionate rates at which black men join the military for socio-economic reasons and the rates at which they are incarcerated, the possibility exists that there are distortions in analyses of female family heads. The major thrust of the Moynihan report, for example, is the pathology of "female-family-headedness."[9]

Despite their limitations, census data serve as crude estimates and generate hypotheses about what is happening in the black community.

There are in the United States an estimated 25,000,000 black persons. They live in 8,000,000 households, 5,905,000 of which are family households.

The 1978 median income of all American families was $17,640. For black families it was $10,879. In 1978, the official poverty income of a nonfarm family of four was established at $6,662. There were a total of 24.5 million persons living below that level. Almost a third of these poor persons were black; and almost a third of black persons were poor, that is, below this poverty level (see table 3.1).[10]

TABLE 3.1   U.S. Population, Black Population, and
Percentage Black by Poverty Status, 1978

	U.S. Persons (thousands)	Black Persons (thousands)	Percentage of Black Persons
All Income Levels	215,856	24,956	11.4
Poverty Level	24,497	7,625	31.1
Percentage at Poverty Level	11.4	30.6	

Source: Adapted from U.S. Department of Commerce, Bureau of the Census, *Characteristics of the Population Below the Poverty Level: 1978.*

There is convincing evidence that families with considerably more income than poverty level income are poor. Kenniston notes that American families tend to perceive poverty as being about half the median income.[11] This means that families of four with incomes of almost $9,000 would still be seriously deprived. Data indicate that 42.1 percent of black families have incomes below $9,000, and 27.5 percent live with incomes below the official poverty level. They are more than three times as likely as all American families to be in poverty (see table 3.2).[12]

TABLE 3.2   U.S. Families and Black Families by
Poverty Status, 1978

	U.S. Families (thousands)	Black Families (thousands)
All Income Levels	57,804	5,905
Below Poverty	5,280	1,622
Percentage Below Poverty	9.1	27.5

Source: Adapted from U.S. Department of Commerce, Bureau of the Census, *Characteristics of the Population Below the Poverty Level: 1978.*

Families with children are likely to be the poorest of all black families (see table 3.3).[13] Families headed by women with children are likely to be the poorest of all. Of all black families below the official poverty level, 75 percent are families of women with children. There are 9,298,000 black children in families; 46.6 percent of them are in families with incomes of less than $9,000, and 36 percent are in families with less than $7,000 in income. Clearly, almost one-half of America's black children are poor.

Although families of women with children make up about 35 percent of black families, the modal black family pattern is the husband-wife family. In March, 1979, 54.9 percent of all black families were husband-wife families. Of these, 58.3 percent had children under eighteen. Families headed by women are much more likely to have children, however; 70.4 percent have children

TABLE 3.3   Median Income in All Black Families by Number
of Related Children

	Total	No Children	1 Child	2 Children	3 Children	4 Children	5 Children	6 Children
Black Families (thousands)	5,905	1,746	1,522	1,262	683	401	147	144
Median Income (dollars)	10,879	11,951	11,603	10,688	10,784	7,725	8,474	9,162

Source: Adapted from U.S. Department of Commerce, Bureau of the Census, *Characteristics of the Population Below the Poverty Level: 1978* and *Money Income of Families in the United States: 1978.*

Notes: Total number of children in black families is 9,298,000.

Median income of all black families with children is $9,855.

under eighteen. More than one-half of black mother-headed families are likely to have had their families disrupted by divorce or separation from their spouses. Thirty percent are single. As few as one percent have husbands who are absent because of their armed-forces affiliations. Another 48,000 women have husbands absent for other reasons. With 47 percent of all the men in state and federal prisons in the United States being black (143,376), it is likely that some of these women and children find their husbands and fathers among the incarcerated (see table 3.4).[14]

TABLE 3.4   Children under 18 in Black Mother-
Headed Families, by Mother's
Marital Status

Mother's Marital Status	Children under 18 (thousands)	Percentage of Children under 18
Single	1,101	30.1
Husband Absent	1,339	36.7
In Armed Forces	27	0.8
Separated	1,264	34.6
Other	48	1.3
Widowed	385	10.6
Divorced	824	22.6
Total	3,649	100.0

Source: Adapted from U.S. Department of Commerce, Bureau of the Census, *Marital Status and Living Arrangements: March 1979.*

Although the income of all black Americans is low relative to the rest of the American population, the income of persons in black families headed by women is four times as likely to be below the official poverty level as is the income in black families headed by men.

To balance the picture, it is fair to argue that *all* black families are not poor. In fact, 13.4 percent of all black families have incomes of over $25,000. Twenty-six percent of black families are above the national median income although 66 percent of these families have wives in the labor force. American families in general who are above the median in income have 54 percent of their wives in the paid labor force.

Although the aggregate income of black families in the United States is 79.2 billion dollars, black families must be characterized accurately as relatively disadvantaged. That is, 73 percent of all black families are below the national median income; 93 percent of all black families *headed by women* are below the national median. And, even where black families are intact, and both spouses are in the labor force, 46 percent have incomes below the national median.

Although the average number of children in all black families is 1.54, 30 percent of black families have children. Close to one-half of these children live in families with just one parent. Most of the one-parent families are families headed by women. The median income of black families with children that are headed by women is $5,366—one-half of the median for all black families and just 30 percent of the national median.

How, then, do black families fare in America? How do they date, mate, procreate, and socialize their children?

NOTES

1. U.S. Department of Commerce, Bureau of the Census, *Money Income of Families and Persons in the United States: 1978.* Washington, D.C.: U.S. Government Printing Office. June, 1980.

2. See Robert B. Hill, *Informal Adoption Among Black Families.* Washington, D.C.: National Urban League Research Department. 1977.

3. See Stack, *All Our Kin.*

4. Ibid.

5. This practice is less frequent since 1966. See U.S. Department of Commerce, Bureau of the Census, *Characteristics of the Population Below the Poverty Level: 1974.* Washington, D.C.: U.S. Government Printing Office. 1976.

6. See, for example, U.S. Department of Commerce, Bureau of the Census, *American Families and Living Arrangements.* Washington, D.C.: U.S. Government Printing Office. May, 1980. Page 9.

7. See U.S. Department of Commerce, Bureau of the Census, *Household and Family Characteristics: March 1979.* Washington, D.C.: U.S. Government Printing Office. July, 1980. Page 103.

8. See U.S. Department of Commerce, Bureau of the Census, *Marital Status and Living Arrangements: March 1979.* Washington, D.C.: U.S. Government Printing Office. February, 1980.

9. Moynihan, *The Negro Family.*

10. U.S. Department of Commerce, Bureau of the Census, *Characteristics of the Population Below the Poverty Level: 1978.* Washington, D.C.: U.S. Government Printing Office. July, 1980.

11. Kenneth Kenniston and the Carnegie Council on Children, *All Our Children: The American Family Under Pressure.* New York: Harcourt Brace Jovanovich. 1977.

12. U.S. Bureau of the Census, *Characteristics of the Population Below the Poverty Level: 1978.*

13. Ibid.

14. U.S. Bureau of the Census, *Marital Status and Living Arrangements: March 1979.*

4

Mating

Little is known of the norms and values regarding black mating. To some extent, who mates whom is influenced by those universals—residential propinquity, race, religion, and social class. But, for the most part, the cultural imagery surrounding the mating process is not in keeping with the characteristics of the culture of a large segment of Afro-American reality. Culturally and historically, large numbers of black Americans have been taught to value the male-female bond. This value for many has been independent of the value placed on material and economic well-being. Several researchers have analyzed black mating within an economic framework and, in doing so, have ignored the affectional aspects of the relationships and have not elicited the value of affection among the people they studied.[1] Marriage rates have persisted among blacks despite economic disincentives and despite economic obstacles to marital success. The correlation of spouses' social classes has not been as high among blacks as among whites. Several researchers have noted that black males will maintain other functional ties and affectional ties to the family, but will move to the economic periphery when the family is under economic stress.[2] Some will become statistically absent[3] or live away from the family completely. If, as in the wider society, the black woman seeks a mate from a "good" family, since it is unlikely to be a criteria of a "good" family, then we need also to know what are the criteria of a "good" family, since it is unlikely to be a monied family of long standing, as it may be in the non-Black community.

Assuming that a human mandate to survive includes an imperative to love, to procreate, and to parent, and that this mandate is shared by most of humanity, then courtship, dating, mating, and procreation are at root unproblematic. Anthropological and archaeological evidence suggest, however, that survival of one person or group has often been at the cost or sacrifice of another person or group, suggesting that universal human survival may have become a subordinate value. Modern rationalizations for survival have followed a tautological evolutionary model, which argues the fittest have survived and will survive. The fittest are purportedly those with an adaptive strength that enables them to have greater reproductive success than those without this capacity. The most accepted theory of human genesis is, therefore, an exclusionary one—one that acknowledges and assigns value to human variation and suggests that variation will be a necessary concommitant to other human activity, including dating, mating, and procreation.

This variation is evident throughout the animal kingdom. All mammals mate, some monogamously. Some mates share a mutual territory and sleep in proximity. Others do not. There are varying degrees of parenting exhibited by mothers and fathers and varying degrees of male and female dominance. These forms of behavior are always related to the ecology of the creature. While at the core of the universe there may be a monolithic thrust of all life toward reproductive success, such success will be variously defined in quantity and quality and in relation to the world of the being. The definition we give to our world, our world view, is, therefore, suggested to be the single most important determinant of the stage on which the drama of individual life will be played out.

Imagine then, the social scientific concern with African tribal society and later Afro-American society being guided by a puritanical belief in the values of continence, restraint, marital sanctity, and hard work. It is no wonder then that tribal and black society were seen as savage, uncivilized, unrestrained, bold, and hedonistic (all with negative connotations). It was in such an intellectual context that much of the "Negro problem" of the twentieth century was attributed to the roving, promiscuous, irresponsible sex life, and fertility of the black American.[4] While such a position defies sensibility for its blatant ignorance of the historical factors that supported, encouraged, and valued black fertility, the underlying assumptions of the poverty of love, sex, and intimacy are even more devastating. In any case, much of the research cited on black intimacy pertains to sexual interaction outside of marriage and devalues it. These researchers assume this sexual interaction is not problematic among the black married and, therefore, do not study it as a problem.

PREMARITAL STUDIES

Studies of sexual permissiveness have sought answers to the "Negro problem" in defining the propensity to reproduce as pathological.[5] Perhaps, without realizing the "damned-if-you-do, damned-if-you-don't" quality of these propositions, black poverty is blamed on black fertility—although black survival may also be blamed. Black fertility is attributed to black irresponsibility, extreme carnality, and casual orientation toward sex.

Black adolescents have been compared to white adolescents,[6] to midwesterners,[7] and to Scandinavians,[8] to test several hypotheses that flow from the Judeo-Christian tradition.[9]

One of the most often cited studies of premarital sexual permissiveness scales permissiveness from kissing when engaged, feeling strong affection, and feeling no affection; to petting; and finally to coitus under the same conditions as described with kissing.[10] The study finds that by these measures blacks are more permissive than whites. This finding was a major source of support for theories of the "sexually irresponsible" black who is to be blamed for his/her own impoverished condition. There are several bases on which a study of this type might have drawn criticism and on which these attitudes might be influenced by socio-economic status. It is very likely that sexual rewards are used to exact conformity with cultural norms, since sexual norms are cultural norms.

A reanalysis of the same data dispelled this criticism.[11] After controlling for social class, a researcher found that black youth were still more permissive than white youth. The researcher noted that sexual permissiveness increased with the number of times whites had been in love. There was no such apparent association for black youth. He interpreted these data as indication that blacks do not need love as a basis for sexual relations. He further attributed this finding to a casualness in sexual affairs engendered by slavery. An equally valid interpretation might be that whites tend to rationalize their sexual behavior by saying they are in love.

Such a focus and interpretation raises such questions as:

1. What is the evidence of such a historical legacy?
2. Why is the concern with youth as opposed to older adults?
3. What is it that makes the researcher focus on black sexuality vis-à-vis white sexuality?

HISTORICAL EVIDENCE

A family textbook that is widely used in family and sociology courses traces the roots of the black family to slavery and describes what the author calls the "demoralization" of the black family.[12] The author of the textbook explains black male-female relations in the Reconstruction era:

> On the plantation the owner had seen to it that the slave mother had a measure of economic security. Now she was forced to depend for support on the Negro male who simply had no tradition of family responsibility. As a consequence, the Negro female was in an intolerable position. She found herself saddled with the burden of supporting *and* rearing the children, while the Negro male availed himself of sexual privileges at the same time repudiating any economic responsibility for family maintenance.[13]

In discussing this statement, Kephart argues that over the years this pattern continued to characterize the black family system.

When we examine the source of this researcher's support we find that he cites and quotes the work of J. C. Furnas. In his *Goodbye to Uncle Tom*,[14] Furnas discusses the slave male as a creature produced by slavery, without motivation or morals: "It follows and the evidence agrees that his principal recreation was sexual intercourse."[15] Such discussions of black families appear over and over again in family textbooks despite efforts to correct these interpretations.[16] They provide the theoretical contexts of many research efforts, but they are not empirically based.

THE FOCUS ON BLACK YOUTH

Concern with black youth may be more a matter of the availability of a captive audience than it is of a scholarly attempt to understand something about youths' sexuality. Without questioning the cultural content of the scales discussed above, the historical explanations, or the assumptions implied in the concern with premarital sexual permissiveness, other researchers have used the scales with high school students. Harrison modified the scales to ask eighty-three white and forty-nine black rural, Mississippi youth whether "petting" was acceptable if in love, feeling strong affection, or feeling no affection; and if coitus was acceptable when in love and when feeling no affection.[17] He also found blacks more permissive than whites. The differences, he said, are due to differences between the permissiveness of black and white females. Again, permissiveness is interpreted pathologically, implying that petting and coitus are bad, but are less bad when in love and worse without love or affection, or either. An interesting but un-interpreted finding in the data is that black youth were apparently more favorable toward coitus if in love or engaged than they were toward petting without affection. It may mean that all such sexual interaction has an affectional basis among the black youth in the sample. In any case, it raises questions about the utility of trying to understand the meaning such interaction has to those being studied and the relationship it bears to love and emotion.

Measurement of the sexual deviation of black youth has been against a norm of white "chastity," which, although it may exist for white youth, is unheard of for the pubescent in traditional African culture. There is some evidence that such a norm functions well within the reward system of a materially oriented society. Those who delay their adulthood in the pursuit of higher education and status have, in exchange for the expression of their sexuality and procreative propensities, greater access to the material rewards of a society. There are those in society, however, who being disenfranchised from total participation in the economic system have an African cultural tradition that values such nonmaterial domains as love, sex, intimacy, and parenting. Consistent with the need of everyone for worth and self-esteem, nonmaterial societies are likely to measure their wealth in offspring and old age. The poor have more children,[18] not because they are ignorant, but because they have to have something that gives meaning to their lives.[19] This interpretation is supported by reduced fertility among members of disadvantaged groups who have achieved economic mobility. Those who are rewarded by status, education, and money have incentive for conformity to norms of chastity, contraception, and monogamous marital sex.

Broderick devised a scale of heterosexual orientation to match up black and white differences in orientation toward the opposite sex.[20] His sample consisted of 1,262 youth in the age range ten to seventeen. Although his black sample differed considerably from his white sample, he did not attempt to determine whether any differences in the findings came from the relative disadvantage of the black sample. Thirty-five percent of the black youth were from broken families, compared to thirteen percent of the white youth. There were twice as many ''only children'' among whites as among blacks. Families with one child only, even in black families, were relatively more advantaged (see table 3.3). There were twice as many blacks as whites with both brothers and sisters. Theoretically, at least, having siblings of one sex or another might influence gender orientation.

Social heterosexuality scores were based on: (1) youth plans for marriage someday, (2) perceptions of heterosexual interaction in a movie scene, (3) whether the youth had a girlfriend (boyfriend), (4) whether the youth has a member of the opposite sex among best friends, (5) whether the youth has ever played kissing games, kissed someone seriously, had a date, or (6) if the youth has ever gone steady, how many times. The researcher found that blacks, as measured, had significantly more positive orientation toward the opposite sex in the age range twelve to thirteen as manifest by their having played kissing games, kissed seriously, dated, and gone steady. There were no differences in orientation toward marriage at this age. In the age group sixteen to seventeen, black youth were significantly less positive toward marriage than white youth. The researcher interpreted this finding as indication that "Negro males are higher in levels of preadolescent sexual interest, but become progressively disillusioned."[21] He concludes, "it seems probable that high levels of unemployment among Negro males help to make the acceptance of family responsibility unattractive. The prominence of matrifocal family patterns among lower-class Negro families might also contribute to the negative attitude toward marriage these data reveal."[22]

These interpretations are exemplary of the lack of theoretical guidance and consequent post hoc explanations used by students of the black family. Certainly, the investigator had no basis for such conclusions since he did not examine the influences of family employment status, "matrifocality," or even social class. This type of research only serves to perpetuate myths regarding the sexual and family patterns of blacks. Note also that conclusions from this study, like the other studies reviewed, are cited uncritically by other researchers.

Dickinson,[23] citing Frumkin's position[24] that changes are occurring among black lifestyles in the direction of assimilating dominant group patterns that blacks aspire to emulate, compared changes in the dating behavior of black and white adolescents between 1964 and 1974. He interprets the increased participation of blacks in activities, such as movies and driving around, which require money, as evidence for racial rather than socio-economic changes. Dickinson acknowledged, but did not examine, the influence of the increased socio-economic status of many blacks between those years.

Independent of those obvious biases of race, class, and culture that have influenced the concern with sexuality among black youth, there is the issue of conceptualization. That petting and coitus should be placed on one continuum representing degrees of sexual interaction is suspect. The context of the petting act may permit only "technical virginity,"[25] and attitudes toward such content can be highly variant culturally. More questionable is the political use of these studies and the way they function to establish intergroup relations.

Pope and Knudsen[26] argue that commitment to norms of chastity functions to maintain the prestige of the advantaged group, while such norms also help to define the disadvantaged as immoral, as the undeserving poor. In the case of Afro-Americans, the use of these norms in social science research has often given scientific credibility to the ill-conceived post-Reconstruction stereotypes of blacks that are made popular by those whose goals are to deny them their human rights.

Kirkendall[27] argues that conventional morality should not be invoked at all, as it is often when studying the premarital sexual experience, but, rather, the researcher should be interested in the effects of sex on the interpersonal relationship. Further, "very immoral experiences" may occur in the realm of sexual behavior without any overt sexual act's having occurred.

THE MYTH OF BLACK AND WHITE SEXUALITY

When viewed in the light of the theories proferred by revisionist historians,[28] and the findings of slave culture with roots in African philosophical systems and culture, the following concerns are raised:

1. Why should the providing for and rearing of black children have been "burdensome" to black mothers during Reconstruction, when, during slavery, they had this responsibility in addition to the duties imposed by their status as slaves? Motherhood is one of the most desired statuses earned in African culture, and child rearing is shared and unburdensome.
2. Why should "sexual intercourse" with black males not be sought and desired by black females? There is no evidence that this was not the case both before and after slavery. Yet every discussion I have ever read of the pre- and post-slavery experience assigns to black women a passive role in sexual relations with white and black males, both of

whom are claimed to exploit them. The historical evidence of their exploitation by the former is patent. The evidence of the sexually exploitative black male, when traced from source to source, is scant, however, and can be traced to the folklore and mythology that maintained slavery and buttresses contemporary racism.[29]

The myth of black male sexuality has supported some of the most brutal treatment of the black male imaginable, while the myth of black female sexuality made her prey to the whims and perversions of white males who afforded her "economic security." Between 1884 and 1900 more than 2,500 black men were lynched, the majority of whom were accused of sexual interest in white women.[30] The myths have been so validated in scientific and other arenas as to give them a reality of their own. Black men who have been denied identities as providers and adequate workers and who have been appreciated for nothing except their sexual prowess have had to embrace this identity often.

A reanalysis that considers Christensen's Scandinavian, midwestern, and Southern black data did not find consistent support for the earlier findings.[31] However, black females were more negative than others toward their first coital experiences, and black males were more likely than any other race/sex grouping to report having had at least six partners and to have had their first coital experience with women to whom they were not committed to marriage or going steady. Johnson suggests that, to some extent, black males may have internalized myths of their supersexuality and may tend to respond or behave along those dimensions.

Myth becomes reality. The truth is that black and white sexuality have the same origins. Potence is stimulated by tenderness and caring and by feelings of adequacy. Folklore surrounding sex and sexuality may have us looking in the wrong place for the answers to male-female harmony.

The bad feelings that women have around first coitus may flow more from actual physical pain and an ignorance of the physiology of sex than from guilt and fear, as some researchers suggest.[32]

One wonders also of the extent to which the concerns of social scientists with black sexuality are projections of their own problems and are not the problems of the people they study. As a case in point, Schulz, in his concern with the sexual behavior of young people in a St. Louis housing project, interviews a young girl, Dora, who denies having had a sexual experience and who says she believes that it is not right to have one yet.[33] Schulz says, "Dora is young and one has the feeling that if the right time and place presented themselves, she would have no objections to doing it."[34] He reacts to the "graffitied" project walls. "Such drawings abound on the stairway walls of the project and together with the many verbal ejaculations in lipstick and crayon announce to all passers-by that sex is very much a central concern of those who live here."[35] I realize that Schulz has seen the "handwriting on the wall." But, that alone is insufficient evidence to support his generalization.

As popular and assumed as are notions about this area of black life, it is amazing to find so large a deficit in the quality and quantity of research. As seen from the methodological poverty and inconclusiveness of research in this area, little definitive and/or meaningful can be said about the differences between blacks and whites. Whether in fact, such differences, if they exist, present a sociological problem is another issue. What contribution to our knowledge will discerning the differences or nondifferences make? Research for such trivial information is symptomatic of another problem—that of the middle-class bias of the social scientist. Copeland argues "whenever one social class looks down upon another as inferior, members of the other are regarded as brutish in nature and vulgar— invariably these inferior classes who are regarded thus are also characterized as dirty and immoral, and contact with them is repugnant."[36] Such a "scientific" position may unwittingly aid and abet the antiscientific position of the bigot, racist, or both.

A major conclusion that flows from a review of this research is that without cautious examination of their own biases, assumptions, and motives, researchers serve, however unwittingly, to perpetuate unfounded stereotypes, and, in doing so, they give scientific validity to racism.

One wonders where history would have taken us, if, with their other powers, the sexual energies of black men had been entrapped in strong, unloved bodies. The very stability of American society may be attributable to the healing sex and intimacy of loving black women.

NOTES

1. David A. Schulz, "The Role of the Boyfriend in Lower Class Negro Life." In Robert Staples, ed., *The Black Family: Essays and Studies.* Second edition. Belmont, Calif.: Wadsworth. 1978. Pages 72-76.

2. Ford, "Case Studies."

3. Stack, *All Our Kin.*

4. See Alan P. Bell, "Black Sexuality: Fact and Fancy." In Robert Staples, ed., *The Black Family: Essays and Studies.* Second edition. Belmont, Calif.: Wadsworth. 1978. Pages 77-80.

5. Ira Reiss, "Premarital Sexual Permissiveness Among Negroes and Whites." *American Sociological Review.* 29:688-698. 1964.

6. Ibid.

7. Harold T. Christensen, "Cultural Relativism and Premarital Sex Norms." *American Sociological Review.* 25:31-39. 1960.

8. Ibid.

9. See Leanor B. Johnson's reanalysis of Christensen data. "The Sexual Behavior of Southern Blacks." In Robert Staples, ed., *The Black Family: Essays and Studies.* Belmont, Calif.: Wadsworth. 1978. Pages 80-93.

10. Reiss, "Premarital Sexual Permissiveness."

11. Ibid.

12. William M. Kephart, *The Family, Society and the Individual.* Third edition. Boston: Houghton Mifflin. 1978.

13. J. C. Furnas, *Goodbye to Uncle Tom.* Quoted in Kephart, *The Family.*

14. Ibid.

15. Ibid.

16. Marie Peters, "Black Family: Perpetuating the Myths. An Analysis of Family Sociology Textbook Treatment of Black Families." *Family Coordinator.* 23:349-357. 1974.

17. Danny E. Harrison, Walter H. Bennett, and Gerald Globetti, "Attitudes of Rural Youth Toward Premarital Sexual Permissiveness." *Journal of Marriage and the Family.* 31:783-787. 1969.

18. See Table 3.3, for example.

19. See Joyce A. Ladner, *Tomorrow's Tomorrow: The Black Woman.* New York: Doubleday Anchor. 1972.

20. Carlfred Broderick, "Social Heterosexual Development Among Urban Negroes and Whites." *Journal of Marriage and the Family.* 27:200-203. 1965.

21. Ibid.

22. Ibid. Page 203.

23. George E. Dickinson, "Dating Behavior of Black and White Adolescents Before and After Desegregation." *Journal of Marriage and the Family.* 37:602-608. 1975.

24. Robert M. Frumkin, "Attitudes of Negro College Students Toward Intrafamily Leadership and Control." *Marriage and Family Living.* 16:252-253. 1954.

25. Hallowell Pope and Dean D. Knudsen, "Premarital Sexual Norms, The Family and Social Change." *Journal of Marriage and the Family.* 27:314-323. 1965.

26. Ibid.

27. Lester A. Kirkendall, *Premarital Intercourse and Interpersonal Relationships.* New York: Julian Press. 1961.

28. See Gutman, *The Black Family*; Eugene Genovese, *Roll Jordan Roll: The World the Slaves Made.* New York: Pantheon. 1974.; Blassingame, *The Slave Community.*

29. See Bell, "Black Sexuality."

30. John Hope Franklin, *From Slavery to Freedom.* New York: Knopf. 1952.

31. Johnson, "The Sexual Behavior."

32. See, for example, Christensen, "Cultural Relativism."

33. David A. Schulz, *Coming Up Black: Patterns of Ghetto Socialization.* Englewood Cliffs, N.J.: Prentice-Hall. 1969. Page 54.

34. Ibid.

35. Ibid. Page 10.

36. Lewis C. Copeland, "The Negro As A Contrast Conception." In Edgar T. Thompson, ed., *Race Relations and the Race Problem.* Durham, N.C.: Duke University Press. 1939.

5

Unwed Motherhood

As serious as the dearth in our knowledge of love and intimacy is our ignorance of the values underlying black procreation, fecundity, and fertility. When viewed from the perspective of a European philosophical system, in which the offspring of a sanctioned union are legal heirs to power and property, the proliferation of a propertyless, black American mass is problematic. Further complicating the issue is the fact that fecundity was valued and encouraged during an earlier period when the offspring of black slaves represented additional chattel.[1] The concentration of the Moynihan report on rates of unwed motherhood among black women as a major source of community pathology reflects the postbellum attitude that black fertility is no longer beneficial to the ruling classes.[2] It is also a reality that a well-documented relationship exists between poverty and fertility. Economic mobility is difficult to accomplish with a large family. Black families with the largest numbers of children are the poorest (see table 3.3). However, children have always been the wealth of the poor, especially in societies and cultures that are less materially oriented.

Rising rates of single parenthood are cited with alarm by social scientists and policymakers. There are 1.1 million children in never-married, single parent families. Only 3 percent of these families are headed by males. Black children in mother-only families are more disadvantaged economically than others. In March, 1979, never-married women in families with children had a median income of $6,161.[3] It is cause for alarm that almost one-half of these children will live in families with incomes below the official poverty level and that one-third of them are preschool age.[4] Black children born to single parents are at a serious disadvantage. There are, therefore, several social consequences of illegitimacy.

Research in the area of illegitimacy has as its most decisive conclusion the fact that higher rates exist for blacks than for whites.[5] Whether these rates flow from culture, sexual behavior, contraceptive use, abortion, reporting, or value placed on babies, is a matter of debate.

There have been several explanations for the higher rates of unwed parenthood in the black community, including: (1) ignorance of the relationship between sex and procreation,[6] (2) ignorance of contraceptives,[7] (3) ineffective use of contraceptives,[8] (4) resistance to racial genocide,[9] and (5) cultural orientations toward abortion, parenting, children, adoption, and contraceptives.[10]

Ladner studied a lower-class black community and observed that young black women view their sexual behavior as natural. They often value reproduction as an act that may or may not be linked to a conjugal tie. As a consequence, Ladner maintains, the concept of illegitimacy is a meaningless one to the people in the community she studied.[11]

Schulz, in his study of ten poor black families in Saint Louis, attributes illegitmacy among young black women to their adaptation to nonurban lifestyles, their uninformed "sex-play," and the incorporation of children into the families of their grandparents, especially grandmothers.[12]

Christensen suggests from the comparison of Scandinavian societies that groups defined as more sexually permissive are also more accepting of premarital pregnancy and, as a result, are less motivated to marry subsequent to such pregnancy.[13]

Other investigators have not found cultural support for premarital pregnancy among blacks. Rather, they find there is rarely rejection of the child through abortion or adoption. Himes, for example, finds that the responses of one hundred black college women to a hypothetical premarital pregnancy revealed that they are very much aware of and sympathetic to the dominant cultural view of such behavior.[14] These women felt that such a pregnancy would incur strong disapproval by formal institutions, including their school, but, at the same time, they felt they would receive acceptance and support from their more intimate associates.

Illegitimacy does not flow from lower-class values, except as these do not incorporate abortion. Furstenberg interviewed 337 pregnant girls and 306 of their mothers, 96 percent of whom were black.[15] Forty-seven percent of this group of girls were from female-headed households, and 80 percent were from homes in which the head was either unemployed or held unskilled or service jobs. He found overwhelmingly that the initial response of these girls to their pregnancies was one of disappointment and awareness that they had violated their family and significant others' expectations. As Himes's coeds reacted to the *hypothetical* case, these lower-class girls' *real* experience was subsequent acceptance and support from their intimates.[16]

Kuvelesky found that black girls in his study had relatively the same hopes for marriage and motherhood as did white girls in his sample.[17] Very few black girls desired marriage before age twenty and most expected to have fewer children than whites.

Contradictions in the research findings are real and are symptomatic of what Herzog labels the "snapshot" approach.[18] That is, a view of a mother after the birth of a child may elicit responses to her pregnancy that are conditioned by the child's being an active and reactive human being. A view of her immediately subsequent to conception might yield quite different information. The incorporation of longitudinal perspectives into the analysis of illegitimacy and unwed parenthood would facilitate observations of stages of the parenting life cycle and inform the development of effective support systems.

Because researchers tend to take an "either-or" approach to interpreting social phenomena, rarely are bicultural influences considered as alternatives. Evidence that bicultural influences may be operating in the area of illegitimacy can be found in several instances. Himes[19] and Furstenberg[20] find that decisions resulting from pregnancy were not in line with the dominant cultural view. Subjects in both studies were unlikely to marry for purposes of legitimation. They preferred to keep their children and did not consider abortion a favorable option. It is apparent that the young women shared the prescriptions of both black and white cultures.

Pope also studied differential decisions regarding illegitimate children made by blacks and whites.[21] He interviewed all of the white and one-third of the black unwed mothers recorded in the public records of selected counties. Half of the whites and two-thirds of the black mothers were from families of semi-skilled and unskilled laborers and sharecroppers. He found that black mothers less often relinquished or were less often advised by others to relinquish illegitimate children through adoption or placement with kin, and they less often considered abortion. He found that black mothers less often married or desired marriage with the fathers of their children if marriage had not been planned before pregnancy. He also found that black unwed mothers had more contact with and financial support from the fathers of their children.[22]

Black women, he argues, perceive fewer advantages from marriage than from single status. They receive fewer rewards for moving toward marriage, and they may not have as normative an orientation toward married motherhood and marital sexual relations as whites.[23]

While Pope's data do show differences in black and white behavioral patterns, the basis for these interpretations is not among the data. Both blacks and whites in his sample have all had premarital sexual relations, and they are all pregnant. His data tell us nothing as to why some sought marriage and others did not. Since he did not control the socio-economic factor, we cannot even tell whether it was those with greater resources who were more likely to marry.

As conclusive as the fact is that higher rates of illegitimacy are recorded for blacks than whites is the fact that one of illegitimacy's correlates is poverty. Whether illegitimacy is a cause, effect, or both, of such poverty is yet to be substantiated. Chilman and Sussman argue that rather than attaching cultural valuation to the behaviors that are increasing the incidence of mother-headed households, researchers need to be more concerned with elucidating the avenues that may be taken toward uplifting this group economically.[24]

Hofferth[25] and Furstenberg[26] challenge the belief that unplanned childbirth in adolescence leads inevitably to a life of disadvantage. Hofferth compared women of twenty-seven years who had their first birth as teenagers with those who were in their early twenties at first birth to examine the influence of age at first birth on their economic well-being. Delays in childbearing did not increase the educational level significantly for blacks as it did for whites. In fact, women who bore children earlier entered the labor force sooner and, as a result, had longer earning careers.

Clearly, unwed motherhood is a fact of life in this last half of the twentieth century.[27] Rises in the rates in which non-black women choose to head their families are again suggesting that motherhood is a condition to be acknowledged independent of matrimony and male parenting. Between 1970 and 1979, there was a 34.7 percent increase in the number of women maintaining families with children and without spouses. What needs to be considered, then, is if there are missing elements in parenting under these conditions, what are they, and how can we compensate for their absence. If need be, can we train unwed mothers to "father" their children, and fathers to "mother"?

NOTES

1. See Eleanor de Almeida [Engram], "Whose Values? Racial Chauvinism in Research on Black Families." *The Black Sociologist.* 6(1):9-24. 1977.

2. Moynihan, *The Negro Family.*

3. U.S. Department of Commerce, Bureau of the Census, *Money Income of Families and Persons in the United States: 1978.*

4. Ibid.

5. See Moynihan, *The Negro Family*; Rainwater, "Some Aspects"; and Pope, "Premarital Sexual Norms."

6. Schulz, *Coming Up Black.*

7. Ibid.

8. Joyce White, "Single Motherhood." In Robert Staples, ed., *The Black Family: Essays and Studies.* Second edition. Belmont, Calif.: Wadsworth. 1978.

9. William Darity and Castellano Turner, "Family Planning, Race Consciousness, and the Fear of Racial Genocide." In Robert Staples, ed., *The Black Family: Essays and Studies.* Second edition. Belmont, Calif.: Wadsworth. 1978.

10. Ladner, *Tomorrow's Tomorrow.*

11. Ibid.

12. Schulz, *Coming Up Black.*

13. Christensen, "Cultural Relativism."

14. Joseph S. Himes, "Some Reactions to a Hypothetical Premarital Pregnancy by 100 Negro College Women." *Marriage and Family Living.* 26:344-347. 1964.

15. Frank F. Furstenberg, "Premarital Pregnancy Among Black Teenagers." *Transaction.* 7:52-55. 1970.

16. Ibid.

17. William P. Kuvelesky and A. S. Obodoro, "A Racial Comparison of Teenage Girls Projections for Marriage and Procreation." *Journal of Marriage and the Family.* 34:75-84. 1972.

18. Elizabeth Herzog, "Is There a 'Breakdown' of the Negro Family?" *Social Work.* 11:3-10. 1966.

19. Himes, "Some Reactions."

20. Furstenberg, "Premarital Pregnancy."

21. Hallowell Pope, "Negro-White Differences in Decisions Regarding Illegitimate Children." *Journal of Marriage and the Family.* 31:756-764. 1969.

22. Ibid.

23. Ibid.

24. Catherine Chilman and Marvin B. Sussman, "Poverty in the United States and in the Mid-Sixties." *Journal of Marriage and the Family.* 26:391-395. 1964.

25. Sandra L. Hofferth, "Early Childbearing and Later Economic Well-Being." *American Sociological Review.* 44(5):784-815. 1979.

26. Frank F. Furstenberg, *Unplanned Parenthood.* Glencoe, Ill.: Free Press. 1976.

27. White families headed by women with children increased from 8 to 13 percent of all white families between 1970 and 1978. See U.S. Department of Commerce, Bureau of the Census, *American Families and Living Arrangements.* Special Studies. May 1980.

6

Marriage

Relatively high rates of marital dissolution among black Americans have led to a series of speculations, propositions, and generalizations about black family life, which often have not been empirically grounded. Among the major propositions are those made popular with the Moynihan report of 1965,[1] although Mr. Moynihan used the much more speculative work of Frazier to buttress his position.[2] Based on the 1960 enumeration of 23 percent of black families' being headed by females, the report explained black family disruption as a function of matriarchal culture, which, theoretically, involves the positive valuation of female instrumentality, authority, and power, which in turn causes male subordination in instrumental roles in relationship to females as well as in other roles valued for males in the dominant culture—including work and military occupations. The series of propositions, although based on speculations about the role of an assumed matriarchy, was used to guide research as if such a configuration did, in fact, exist. And so the focus of such research was on the conjugal dyad in isolation from the forces that might impinge upon it.

THE CONJUGAL DYAD

There are approximately 3.5 million black married couples in the United States, and 95 percent of them live together. They live in a socio-economic political context in which:

1. Their median income is just 82.3% of the income of all American families with married couples.[3]
2. Families headed by women are extremely disadvantaged.
3. There are 6,570,000 single black women and 4,786,000 single black men.[4]

These figures include men and women who have as yet never been married or are separated, divorced, or widowed. The imbalance in the ratio of available black males to females is greatest in the age ranges where men and women would be most likely to be seeking mates (see table 6.1). The overall ratio of males to females is just seventy-two to one hundred. In the age range thirty to thirty-four it is just sixty-three to one hundred. These factors apply external pressures to existing stable conjugal dyads.[5]

Imbalances in the sex ratios have existed since the earliest censuses and have been noted by other researchers.[6]

In considering the dimensions along which men and women select their mates, including geographic proximity, education, occupation, employment status, and social class, it is likely that actual availability ratios broaden even further. There were 136,893 black adult males in state and federal prisons at the end of 1978, equaling 47 percent of *all* men in these prisons.[7] The pathologies associated with second-class citizenship, including alcoholism, drug use, stress-related illnesses, and early debility and death, and which are compounded by unemployment, disproportionately affect black males and further reduce the pool of available men.

In response to these conditions, black wives have been in the labor force longer and in greater numbers than have their nonblack counterparts (see table 6.2). These labor force activities have nurtured theories of black women's dominance in their homes and conjugal relations and theories of the pathological black male role.

Research on black conjugal dyads has thus been guided by theories of cultural internalization of these pathological roles, and researchers have attempted to document the matriarchy,

TABLE 6.1 Marital Status in the Nonmarried Black Adult Population, by Age and Sex

	Age and Sex																		
Marital Status	14-17		18-19		20-24		25-29		30-34		35-39		40-44		45-54		55-64		65+	
	M	F	M	F	M	F	M	F	M	F	M	F	M	F	M	F	M	F	M	F
Single	1159	1150	497	514	855	908	352	414	160	193	84	119	88	70	130	74	60	43	57	56
Separated	0	2	0	8	21	77	66	152	87	140	49	113	50	119	87	198	101	96	71	54
Widowed	0	1	0	0	0	0	0	11	4	15	6	39	7	37	57	185	67	322	166	680
Divorced	0	0	0	0	11	21	61	92	52	135	56	118	92	113	114	169	73	82	41	52
Total	1159	1153	497	522	887	1006	481	669	303	483	195	389	237	339	388	626	301	543	335	842

Source: U.S. Department of Commerce, Bureau of the Census, *Marital Status and Living Arrangements: March 1979.*

M = Male
F = Female

TABLE 6.2   Wives Employed Full Time, in
Wife-Present Families, Black and White

	Wife Present (thousands)	Wife Employed Full Time (thousands)	Percentage
Black Families	3,244	1,388	42.8
White Families	43,636	13,511	31.0
All Families	47,692	15,247	32.0

Source: U.S. Department of Commerce, Bureau of the Census, *Marital Status and Living Arrangements: March 1979.*

male-female role reversal, and imbalance in exchange, power, and authority.

Given the propensity of propositions generated in the field of black family study regarding family relationships, the paucity of research on black conjugal units and black family interaction patterns and processes is amazing. The existing research on black conjugal dyads has largely been concerned with husband and wife roles, status relationships, and marital satisfaction. To some extent, this is a function of the inviolability of the privacy of the home and the fact that black families infrequently utilize agencies that collect such data as a matter of course. This does not justify the failure of social scientists to seek the alternate sources of data that would be required for scientific rigor.

ROLE PERFORMANCE AND STATUS

While Moynihan and other investigators have argued that conjugal roles are often reversed in black families, the evidence to substantiate the thesis is slight. In fact, much of the evidence refutes this position.[8]

The major empirical support for black female dominance comes from studies that compared mean power scores of black and white research subjects. One study conducted in Detroit

in 1955 asked wives in 103 black families and 554 white
families to respond to a series of questions regarding who
makes decisions in each of eight spheres.[9] Matriarchy was
attributed to differences in the mean scores on a scale ranging
from ten, husband power, to zero, wife power. It is questionable
whether the difference between 5.2 and 4.4 is either valid
or meaningful. An equally valid interpretation of the same
scores is that they reflect black family egalitarianism and white
patriarchy. Also begging an answer is the question of the
statistical significance between the scores of 5.2 and 4.4. Is
it possible that the differences between the scores are meaningless and, therefore, unworthy of interpretation? Instead the
authors posit that since blacks show more evidence of clinging
to traditional male roles when it comes to helping out around
the house, their sense of "masculinity" may be threatened by
frequent unemployment (of which the husbands in this study
show no evidence) and, thus, they defensively cling to these
roles.[10] This wavering between interpretations to salvage the
theorists' position from the data that contradict it and especially
this tendency to incorporate negative findings and to interpret
them as psychological defense mechanisms reflect what I call
the "damned-if-you-do, damned-if-you-don't" perspective from
which Afro-American behavior has often been described and
interpreted. While it is probably true that unemployment has
a measurable effect on family internal dynamics, the empirical
link has not been made in this research. The attribution of
patriarchal power to psychological defense rather than to the
original dimension being measured sounds like psychological
"denial" on the part of the researcher. Yet for me to make
such an assertion would be "unscientific," since I am not
measuring the quality of the researcher, but the quality of the
research. With respect to the quality of the research, throughout
the study and particularly on page 34 of the report, the researchers,
without presenting supportive data, state "such peculiar reversals
of White trends occur often enough within the Negro community
to lead us to treat Negro families separately throughout this
book." On what evidence are such "peculiar reversals" based?[11]

In addition to the obvious problems in interpretation there are other methodological flaws. For example, failure to use multivariate techniques of analysis prevents the researchers' simultaneous control of all the variables they consider separately when they make their case for black female dominance. It is obvious that race, social class, and female employment are intercorrelated variables and that any analysis of racial effects needs to be controlled statistically. When one considers the impact of the Moynihan report on the interpretations of other investigators, it is startling to discern both the flimsiness of the evidence and the quality of the research that was given credence.[12]

Brink and Harris asked a random sample of blacks and community leaders, "In most families, do you think the mother or father is usually the one who teaches children to behave right?"[13] The investigators interpret the finding that most of the respondents report they think it is the mother as being exemplary of "the matriarchal character of Negro society." Certainly, this type of question given to any group in America would yield the same response, since mothers usually spend more time than fathers with their children. These authors have precluded the possibility of their discerning this finding by focusing on blacks to validate their preconceived notions of matriarchy.

Middleton and Putney compared black and white college professors and skilled laborers to see if these racial and class groups differed in the mothers' or fathers' taking the dominant role in family decisions.[14] Rather than asking "Who decides?" they asked husband and wife to fill out questionnaires, first separately, then jointly. The questions took such form as, "Should toilet training for a child begin before he is one year old?" and "When friends come over, would you prefer to watch television or just sit and talk?" Questions were in the area of child care, purchases and living standards, recreation, and role attitudes.

Disagreements between husband and wife on the individual questionnaires were tabulated, and the proportion of such disagreements that was resolved in favor of the husband's original position on the joint questionnaire was employed as a measure on a continuum between matriarchy and patriarchy. These researchers found no differences between racial and occupational groups. Overwhelmingly, the respondents were egalitarian, that is, just as many joint decisions were resolved toward the wives' original positions as the husbands'. Couples with employed wives were more egalitarian, but, when not, they were twice as likely to be patriarchal whereas couples with unemployed wives when not egalitarian were matriarchal. These conclusions are counter to those based on wife reports rather than on observations of actual joint decisions.[15]

Overwhelmingly, the research communicates an egalitarian roles structure shared by black mates. Some wives expect males to be dominant in decisions, some wives expect husbands to be dominant only in certain decisions.[16] Despite their egalitarian behavior, some wives perceive husbands to be dominant in all decisions.[17] This view may flow from their incorporation of what they believe are their husbands' desires into their own decisions.

Husbands are also likely to perceive themselves as dominant and sometimes attribute more dominance to themselves than their wives attribute to them.[18] The belief that all males should prevail in decisions may be the source of family conflict. Cromwell and Cromwell noted, for example, a low correlation between black male and female perceptions of dominance, although their reported decisions were egalitarian.[19]

What is probably true is that there are domains in which one or the other mate is more likely to prevail in decisions. However, very few decisions are made unilaterally in the black conjugal dyad. Support for the matriarchy is scant.

All mother-present families tend to find women as structurally central. Children are likely to perceive their mothers as dominant in a variety of decisions where fathers would have had influence.

The struggle for survival has characterized black families. Therefore, both fathers and mothers are viewed as sources of support in black families. The dichotomy of roles that has been compatible to white family success has not been an option widely available to black families.

There is some evidence, however, that black women, given certain middle-class resources, are as likely as others to choose to stay home.[20] The option has been less available. Research in this area has assumed and focused on a pathology in the decision making of black dyads. Researchers have not attempted to understand the extent to which the participation of mothers is an asset to the labor force, to their children, to their lifestyles, and to their men. In many ways black women have been at the vanguard of the movement that is freeing white men and women from structurally defined roles. As a consequence, men are coming into new dimensions of their experiences; they are learning to mother as women have learned to father. There has been a 91 percent increase since 1970 in families headed by men with children with no spouse present. There are close to one million children living in families with their father only.[21]

Recommendations to the White House Conference on Families with respect to economic well-being manifest recognition of this development. Husbands and wives are seeking ways in which both can participate in the home and in the labor force.[22] If traditional role prescriptions have required different emotional and personality orientations, then these new families will need help in incorporating the formerly ignored dimensions of their lives. Women will experience role conflict, ambivalence, and sometimes guilt as they leave their homes and enter the labor force. Men will feel less potent as they move into more supportive roles.[23]

The belief that men are instrumental and women expressive is undergoing change. While it is not as yet conclusive that the functional male domain has ever been that of instrumental activity and the female's of expressive activity, this belief has been an assumption underlying much of the research that investigates the effects of maternal employment on male and female roles. The extent of instrumentality versus expressiveness among black men and women was sought as a measure of the personality correlates of matriarchy and female dominance.

Scanzoni, in an investigation of black families whose status positions are above the lower class, reports that two-thirds of his respondents cite their father's aid as being mostly instrumental and their mother's expressive.[24] Based on case studies in a lower-class community, Rainwater has argued that the black male has basically an "expressive" lifestyle, and because of this, black women are forced into more instrumental concerns.[25]

Aldous studied the relationship between wives' employment status and the marital roles of lower-class husbands in black and white stable families.[26] She proposes that the high degree of conjugal role segregation characteristic of the lower class in combination with wife employment would result in less participation by husbands in household tasks. The matriarchal character of black families, she speculates, results in even less participation by black husbands in the home since the effect of the black wives' contribution by way of employment is relatively greater, and pushes husbands further toward the periphery of family affairs.[27] Aldous compared the mean response scores of 122 white and 46 black men on measures of: (1) the extent to which the husband communicates with his wife about a range of problems; (2) his report of his wife's communication with him; (3) the amount of his participation in household and child care tasks; and (4) his participation in family decisions.

The major part of her discussion of her findings deals with her having found *fewer differences* among white men than among black men in participation, whether their wives were employed or unemployed. Thus she skirts her original question of whether the racial groups differ. The answer indicated by her data is that they differ considerably, but more interesting is *how* they differ. The only significant differences are that without respect to the wife's employment status:

1. Black men were *more* likely to take out the garbage.
2. Black women communicate *more* with their husbands about health problems.
3. Black men communicate *more* with their wives about work problems, feeling depressed, and health problems.[28]

Among the interaction effects, the data indicate that:

1. Black husbands with employed wives have less power than white husbands with employed wives when it comes to making decisions as to whether to have children.
2. Black employed wives communicate more about money problems.
3. Black husbands have more power in decisions about paying bills when the wife is unemployed, whereas white husbands have more power if the wife is employed.
4. Black husbands have more decisionmaking power regarding the amount to spend on clothing if the wife is unemployed, whereas whites have equal power in this area, regardless of the wife's employment status.

In all other areas, there are no differences between blacks and whites.[29]

From the data, Aldous concludes that there is a statistically nonsignificant trend showing that the black wives' employment status is inversely related to the husbands' "acceptance of family responsibilities, support for the Moynihan thesis."[30] Certainly, this is a gross distortion of the actual findings, and, as so often happens with this type of research, the researcher chooses to focus on those findings that support the thesis and either to ignore or discount the others, although these may be more convincing.

Consistent with the "damned-if-you-do, damned-if-you-don't" perspective, which I have argued is often brought to bear on black family study, Aldous speculates that the data that show greater communication among blacks than among whites in the sample may indicate "problem centered conjugal relations." This speculation is obviously suggested to explain away the negative results, since the original thesis proposed greater communication to be indicative of greater power and of better family relationships. Although the analytical method employed in the study permits a greater capacity for statistical control, the unequal sample size of the black and white men casts additional doubt on the validity of the findings.

INSTRUMENTAL VERSUS EXPRESSIVE
ROLE RELATIONS

Consistent with such theories of the peripheral role of black males, some theorists have examined areas of family life in which they hypothesized black men to be subordinate, as opposed to dominant, in several dimensions in relationship to black women. Babchuck and Ballweg expected lower- and working-class black women to have friends and primary ties, independent of their husbands', and which the wives initiated.[31] This, they say, would be consistent with the more peripheral role expected of black lower-class men. In contrast, they expected middle-class black men to be a greater source of primary ties, reflecting their dominance. They found no differences.

Consistent with the traditional dichotomy of sex roles into male or female, instrumental or expressive, and labor force or home, some theorists have focused on the labor force activity of black women who were presumed to be "out-of-role." Empirical research in this area has examined: (1) attitudes toward working wives,[32] (2) attitudes toward working mothers,[33] (3) children's perceptions of working mothers,[34] (4) ideal family role performance,[35] (5) orientation of young women toward possible adult roles,[36] and (6) differences in male-female instrumentality and expressiveness.[37] For the most part, black men have manifest a degree of comfort with their wives' working. Axelson found that more than two-thirds of black husbands in a sample of Florida men believed wives should work if they desire.[38] Twenty-seven percent felt they should work only in an emergency.

Black men were not as supportive of wives' getting equal pay for equal work, and 40 percent believed men would feel inadequate should their wives earn more money than they. Younger black men were more liberal in their attitudes than men over age thirty.

Black men also felt working wives were poorer companions. Since these attitudes were not analyzed in relationship to the respondents' own situations, several questions remain:

1. Are their variations in comfort with working wives

attributable to the time spent in the labor force by working wives—that is, full versus part time? Women who spend more time at work would be, in fact, lesser companions!
2. Are the black men in the sample receiving lower salaries than their wives? If so, it may be a source of conflict in black families. The structure of sex roles and expectations of men are that they should lead their families in income.
3. Are black men paid equal rates for equal work?

Research on children's perceptions of working mothers and on youth orientations toward instrumental versus expressive traits in their mates, shows black youth attach greater importance to instrumental capacity.[39] Again, this finding may be a function of the conditions of the children in the sample.

Although role prescriptions may flow from white, middle-class norms, other researchers have noted that the economic system modifies and diversifies family roles. Himes observed that household participation varies with the amount and type of occupational participation of his respondents.[40] The study, although the sample is too small and select on which to base generalizations, emphasizes the need to study the relationship between social structure and family interaction processes.[41]

Clearly, the major problem with this area of inquiry is conceptual. The placement of instrumentality and expressiveness at opposite poles of a continuum is perverse. It reflects the duality of being and dichotomy of existence that pervades Western philosophy and is the source of inner conflict and psychic pain.

Men have had to be instrumental at the cost of being expressive and have had to suppress and to deny emotional life. When these feelings have surfaced, they have called into question the basic worth of a man, his masculinity, his adequacy, as a husband, mate, and father.

Likewise, the efficacy of working women as mothers has been questioned as manifest in the proliferation of research on the children of working mothers.[42] Black women were thus put in the "damned-if-you-do, damned-if-you-don't" position of being forced to work for the very survival of their children at the same time as they were blamed for the pathology that was theorized to flow from their working. From their review of the research on working mothers in fatherless families, Herzog and Sudia show clearly that the pathology of working women is in their oppression and exploitation in the labor force as manifest in low salaries, relegation to low status positions, inadequate child care, and inadequate assistance at home.[43]

Black women are more likely to work for money than are white women, although they are at the lowest range in occupational hierarchies.[44] Their husbands are more likely to have lower incomes, and consequently they are less likely to be opposed by their husbands when they do work.[45]

It is apparent that given sufficient resources, black women would be as likely as others to select a homemaking role, but this option has not been as available.[46]

POWER AND AUTHORITY

The belief that authority, that is, legitimate power, should reside in males flows from an ideology that has served to oppress American women and to prescribe their limited roles. This ideology finds women deficient in those qualities that are required for leadership, including family leadership. The qualities in which women are purportedly lacking are: rational, as opposed to emotional, thought processes; assertiveness; competitiveness; and aggression. Ideologically, the prescribed nature of women is: emotional, acquiescent, giving as opposed to taking, and noncompetitive.

Such an ideology supports the relegation of women to supportive roles and creates negative expectations of their abilities to function in circumstances requiring "dominance," "decisiveness," and other "male qualities."

The splitting of sex roles further supports the beliefs that:

1. The locus of power, dominance, and authority should be in just one sex.

2. Males and females are of opposite temperament.
3. Male and female spheres of activity are separate and different.

Therefore, when single women worked in the nineteenth century—when work was strictly construed a male domain of activity—they believed that they were out of their "proper sphere." Wives did not work for fear of creating the impression that their husbands were inadequate.[47]

During that same period a black female labor force was structurally maintained. From this contradictory condition flowed the perceptions of black female dominance, power, authority, and masculinity and black male inadequacy and femininity.

Studies of the black family, black labor force participation, and the socio-economic condition of blacks suggest that the traditional organization of sex roles never did and still does not articulate well with the black experience. The low status of black males in the labor market has made the monetary contributions of black women essential for the economic survival of black families. The income of black working wives increases their median family income by almost one-third.[48] Black women long have worked out of necessity and have combined family with labor market roles. Economic conditions and desires for better living standards always have conflicted with the notion that black women belong in the home and should not participate in productive paid labor. The labor force activity of black women has been comparatively high since the turn of the century in relation to the activity of other American women. While some researchers have suggested this role has been internalized culturally,[49] there is as much evidence to suggest that this continuous labor force activity has been structurally maintained intergenerationally.[50]

Despite the fact that black families would not survive very well without the income of working women, their labor force activities have been called pathogenic by researchers who have tested hypotheses based on social stereotypes. In fact, researchers have argued that the salience of black women in the labor force in a society that values male dominance causes male feelings of inadequacy and poor self-esteem and results in their delinquency, drug use, unemployment, and in their failure in school and on other tests.

Pathology-ridden males are ineffective, thus causing females to become even more important in family and economic affairs and sustaining a cyclical process. While these generalizations have been discredited by many,[51] many other researchers cite them as explanations of differences found between white and black family behavior.[52] While some of the literature has been devoted to the question of the validity of treating black from white statistical deviations as being inherently pathological,[53] little research has addressed the question of whether such a causal chain might exist.

Research on maternal employment that has been directed primarily at the white, middle-class segment of America has shown repeatedly that maternal employment, by itself, has very little explanatory power in relationship to other variables that affect family relationships.

Hoffman, for example, identifies a number of variables that influence the relationship between a mother's employment and other familial phenomena.[54] Among these are socio-economic resources, age of child, sex of child, mother's attitude toward her employment, the adequacy of alternative supervision of her children, urban versus rural residence, and response of the husband or father to her employment.[55] The idea that maternal employment causes personality maladjustment in children has been broadly discredited.[56] Findings from the investigation of the influence of maternal employment on juvenile delinquency suggest that a positive relationship may hold for middle-class, but not for lower-class, families.[57] There have been few studies that attempt to elucidate the patterns in family roles, inter-actions, and sentiments, that accompany maternal employment in black families. Yet popular descriptions of black families would suggest that such has been the case. It is within such a socio-political context that the locus of power in black families has been studied. Propositions regarding power in *all* families are rife with contradiction. The following propositions regarding lower-class families all purportedly find empirical support in the research literature:

1. Lower-class families are more likely to be matriarchal.[58]
2. Lower-class families are more likely to be patriarchal.[59]
3. Lower-class families tend to be more egalitarian.[60]

This confusion gets carried over to research on black families, where black families are found by different researchers to be, at once, matriarchal,[61] egalitarian,[62] and patriarchal.[63] In many cases, the research from which the conclusions flow is of highly questionable quality.

Schwartz compared the perceptions of family authority patterns held by black and white socio-economic subgroups.[64] Although the researcher claims to be drawing on interviews and observations involving 510 black lower-class boys, 100 southern white migrant families, and 30 middle-class black families, none of the discussion is supported by illustrative data. Schwartz is widely quoted and cited by others. He argues that black boys are as likely to perceive their mother as father to be "boss" and compares this to field workers' observations that white fathers appear to be "consistently strong and dominating." He further argues that lower-class boys experience dissonance in their perceptions of family authority patterns due to the fact that they may perceive the mother as having status and the father as having authority. He concludes from this hypothesis that there are "two types of matriarchy in the black community—maladaptive and adaptive." He argues, "The maladaptive situation is one in which status and authority adhere in *two different parties* such that the absent father situation would be more adaptive than that of a present ineffectual father."[65]

If the investigator had evidence for these conclusions, it was not presented. That status and authority need lie in the same parent is an unfounded assumption on the part of the author, and his leap from that assumption to the attribution of dissonance to the youth who perceives the two as shared displays an even faultier logic. Deserving of even greater criticism, however, is the violation of social scientific method, which is reflected in (1) the comparison of the perceptions of black youth of their own family to the field workers' perceptions of white families, (2) the imbalance in the sampling ratios, and

(3) the failure to present illustrative data. The notion of a present, ineffectual father was extended by Schulz in an observational study of residents of a lower-class housing project in Saint Louis.[66] He maintains that black fathers represent poor role models for adolescent males, even when present in the household, since they are ineffectual in the face of their wives' dominance. This study also is uncontrolled by a specific research design, and the interpretations and conclusions also come from largely impression-istic data.

Ladner's study of residents of the same housing project as Schulz's study, although descriptively the same, offers different conclusions.[67] By not focusing on *deviant* roles, she reports a range of male types from stable, present fathers, who exercise strict control over their sons and daughters, to the more "deviant" types whom Schulz proffers as the typical pattern. Ladner's study, like Schulz's because of her methodology, cannot be generalized beyond the group studied, but among the hypotheses generated are that a range of male and family types exists even in lower-class black communities.

Hyman and Reed compare black and white responses to questions purported to measure the balance of power between spouses on three sample surveys: (1) the 1960, Almond and Verba "Civic Culture" data, (2) a 1951 "Gallup" survey, and (3) a Survey Research Center, 1965 Political Socialization study.[68] They find that the percentage of respondents to these three surveys who found either their mother or father most influential when growing up was not significantly different when comparing blacks to whites. The percentage reporting parental decisions about child rearing and important family decisions was not significantly different for black and white respondents, whether they were married or single. The proportions of black respondents who report that either the husband or wife should decide how the pair should vote were not significantly different from the proportions of white respondents responding similarly. Proportions who agreed with either the mother or father in politically divided homes were not significantly dif-ferent between the racial groups. Evidence from this study supports the proposition that if these responses on the average can be considered matriarchal, then both racial groups are matriarchal in character.

Parker and Kleiner theorized that if deviant family performance in the black community is a normative phenomenon, then differences in socio-economic status variables should be associated with differences in expressed "ideals" regarding family role performance.[69] They further theorized that if family role performance is such a subculturally patterned phenomenon, then discrepancies between ideal and actual role performance should not be accompanied by feelings of failure.

To test these propositions, a subsample of black male respondents was taken from a random sample of Philadelphians and compared to a random sample of males from the same city who were diagnosed as mentally ill. Respondents were asked to report first what they perceived as ideal role performances and later their actual family role performance. There was no relationship between the stated ideals and status variables on matters including education, income , occupation, educational, and occupational mobility. This suggests that lower-class subcultural norms do not operate within the group to define role performance. When examining the discrepancy between ideal and actual role performance, there was an inverse relationship between income and the discrepancy, suggesting that the greater the income, the more likely is the man to approach his ideals.

A self-anchored striving scale was administered in which spontaneous responses regarding the man's first thoughts of "the best possible" or "worse possible" way of life were sought.[70] The investigators found that the tendency to mention family relationships in these descriptions was also inversely related to income. This suggests that family concerns are salient in the minds of low-income men. Respondents were asked to place themselves on a continuum between the "best possible" and "worse possible" way of life. There were significant differences between the mentally ill, those whose ideal and actual family roles were inconsistent, and those whose ideal and actual roles were in agreement. The mentally ill were least positive in their assessments of their lives, whereas men whose ideal roles were closest to their real roles felt they had better lives.

The mentally ill were least likely to think they had a chance of accomplishing their ideal life. Conclusions from this study are:

1. Perceptions of ideal family role performance are nearly the same for all status groupings.
2. Deviation from these ideals is associated with low income.
3. Deviation is also associated with an awareness that one is not achieving his goals.
4. This awareness is accompanied by feelings of hopelessness.

While this study does not introduce intervening variables that link mental illness to family role discrepancy, such a link is suggested and is certainly worthy of future exploration. The data also present a convincing argument that differences in family role performance are not subculturally valued and patterned in the black lower class.

Scanzoni studied the structure of sex roles and the conditions that promote or obstruct marital satisfaction in black and white marriages within the context of a five-state, metropolitan area probability sample.[71] The sample of 3,100 included 25 percent black respondents and consisted of marriages in which both spouses were living together and had been married only to each other. Wives in the sample were aged eighteen to forty-four years. Forty-five of the wives in the sample worked full time (no part time or racial distribution given), and husbands comprised approximately half of the sample. Twelve items pertaining to the wife's role were analyzed for men and women. In a factor analysis, two dimensions emerged for both sexes. The first dimension comprised eight items, such as, "a married woman's most important task in life is to be taking care of her husband and children." Scanzoni calls this dimension the "traditional wife" role. Another dimension composed of four items, such as, "having a job herself should be just as important as encouraging her husband in his job," was called "self-actualization." He defines *role modernity* as lesser agreement with the items in the traditional wife scale and greater agreement with the items on the self-actualization scale. Likert-type responses to the items were analyzed as a measure of role traditionalism or modernity.*

He also discerned such dimensions pertinent to what he calls the husband role as (1) "problematic husband alterations," based on the temporary problematic alterations a husband may make in connection with his wife's employment efforts; (2) "institutionalized husband-wife equality," which emphasizes prominent, nontraditional behavior of the husband in response to his wife's employment, and (3) "traditional husband role," in which the items reflect firm role segregation or specialization. Greater and lesser role modernity was also measured by Likert-type responses to the husband role items. Two dimensions of the "maternal role" were extracted for both sexes. The first, "religious legitimation of the mother role," reflected a sacred-secular orientation toward motherhood; the second was the "traditional mother role," in which the interests of children are superordinate to the interests of the mother. Greater modernity of the mother role was measured by Likert-type responses to the items within the dimensions.

Two dimensions of "self-concept," "instrumental" and "expressive," measured self-conceptions regarding activeness, aggressiveness, and task-orientation (instrumental), and nurturance, supportiveness, and person-orientation (expressive). In the final set of items, wives were asked to evaluate themselves and husbands were asked to evaluate their wives as being either very good, good, or poor on eight abilities, both traditional and nontraditional, including "cooking, budgeting, hostessing" and "knowledge and experience necessary to hold a job now or later." These eight items did not separate into two dimensions in a factor analysis, so they were employed in one scale labeled

---

*Likert-type responses are those for which the subject or respondent is asked to indicate his or her agreement or disagreement with a statement. Agreement-disagreement is measured in intensity, for example, *strongly agree, agree, undecided, disagree,* or *strongly disagree.* These responses are scored ordinally so that one end of the scale, for example, *strongly agree,* will be the highest score and the other end will be the lowest score.

"ability evaluation," which measured the perceived skill competency of wives.

Although the researcher expected blacks to be more egalitarian than whites, he found that this was so only with respect to "wife self-actualization," "problematic husband alterations," and "institutionalized equality," which are the more radical departures from traditional preferences. On the more conventional aspects of marital roles, as expressed in the "traditional wife" and "traditional husband" dimensions, blacks were not more egalitarian. As to instrumental and expressive self-concepts, blacks of both sexes tended to perceive themselves as both more instrumental and more expressive than whites. Among the more highly educated there was no difference between the races on measures of "expressive self-concept," and "wives' ability evaluation," while among the lesser educated, blacks remained higher on both expressiveness and ability.

Black wives in this study attribute more authority to themselves and black husbands less authority to themselves than white wives and husbands. Scanzoni concludes from this analysis of sex roles that the evidence indicates that in behavioral terms blacks choose more egalitarian arrangements, while whites select situations and ideologies that are more moderate or neotraditional. One significant finding is that without regard to education, blacks emerge as more "instrumental" in self-concept than whites. In combination with the fact that blacks also rate their wives' abilities higher than whites, this finding would suggest that black males are not made to feel ineffectual by their wives' capabilities, as has been suggested by other researchers.

Other researchers have also noted a higher quality of data flowing from the inclusion of both men and women in studies measuring sex roles. Cromwell and Cromwell's data show that measuring wife's perceptions alone leads to distortion.[72] There is always the possibility when doing this type of study of omitting items that are of importance and that may have emerged in the same dimension. The cost, however, may prohibit such exhaustive inclusion. This study is one of the most complex designs ever undertaken in the study of husband and wife roles and represents a giant step along the continuum from simple to complex studies that seek to answer complex questions.

The area of research regarding black family role performance and status relationships remains highly inconclusive. Many researchers, because they assume status relationships in black families to be *culturally* patterned phenomena, ignore *status* variables in comparing black to white decisionmaking processes.[73] Other researchers, although they may be widely cited in the literature as support for the positions of other investigators, base their conclusions on little more than impressionistic data.[74] While many investigators report that there is no significant difference in the relationships of black and white spouses,[75] many other investigations do report such differences.[76] Conflicting findings probably flow from the differences in methods employed by the researchers. Assumptions, concepts, propositions, theories, and observational methods employed in this area of research vary, mirroring the imprecision in the field.

Aside from other methodological issues and the philosophical issues underlying the research, the problem of interpretive bias remains crucial. Some researchers have failed to consider their *own* evidence when it was counter to their original theoretical positions. The implication, therefore, is that the research effort is not directed toward furthering knowledge. Instead it appears that the effort is meant to validate existing ideology and stereotypes.

MARITAL SATISFACTION

High rates of marital disruption among black Americans, as reflected in rates of divorce and separation, promote concern with the internal dynamics of black families. From the point of view of popular theoretical perspectives, husbands and wives in black families are expected to be lower in levels of satisfaction than are white husbands and wives.

Several researchers have noted a relationship between the marital satisfaction of black husbands and wives and income, sexual satisfaction, and role differentiation. Rainwater noted that couples who emphasized joint activity in the home and outside the home are more interested in sex and enjoy sex more.[77] Satisfactory sex lives, in turn, influence their satisfaction with their marriages. On the other hand, he noted that black couples who maintained highly segregated roles were less interested in sex and less satisfied with their marriages. There is also a documented relationship between fear of pregnancy, sex, and marital satisfaction.[78] Couples who fear conception enjoy sex less and have less rewarding marriages. There is further evidence that children, at least under specified conditions, decrease marital satisfaction. Studies of married men and women from more than four thousand California households revealed that the presence of children decreases satisfaction in the marriages of black and white spouses. Black men with children were more satisfied if their incomes were $10,000 or more, whereas white husbands, regardless of income, were more satisfied without children. Black wives with or without children were less satisfied with their marriages when their husbands made less than $10,000. Both black and white families with children were not as satisfied as those whose children had grown up and left home. Those who never had children were the most satisfied with their marriages. In the study sample 62 percent of black women under forty-five years old worked full time compared to 37 percent of white wives. This work force activity may have combined with the presence of children to lessen black wives' satisfaction with their marriages. This hypothesis, however, was not tested.

Black wives have been shown consistently to be less satisfied with their marriages. Whether it is the marriages per se or factors that influence them is a source of contention among researchers.

Widely cited, but poorly analyzed, data document the differences in marital satisfaction of black and white blue-collar wives in Detroit.[79] Likert-type responses to the question How satisfied are you with your marriage? yield the "least enthusiastic" response from black women. That they are enthusiastic at all should be surprising, given the importance that is assigned to income by everyone and their being the least likely to have any. The investigators compare black women to white women, who are most enthusiastic, and attribute the lack of enthusiasm by black women to being wives to "a deficiency in interaction"—a conclusion for which they have no evidence or data. In fact, there are several analyses that might have contributed to the understanding of differences, but which the researcher did not consider. It appears, instead, that the researchers just wanted to document differences and to interpret them within the existing theoretical frameworks. No analysis attempted to account for the influence of children, although this influence has been related theoretically and empirically to marital satisfaction.

Lopata is widely cited for her case studies of forty-eight housewives in which she reports that black lower-class wives are more hostile toward their husbands than other wives.[80] Just how she arrives at these conclusions is unclear since she reports no supportive data.

In contrast to these widely cited studies, a more recent and much more complex study employed "multiple regression" techniques to examine the way in which education, jobs, age, and religion influence economic satisfaction and marital satisfaction.[81] The strongest predictor of economic satisfaction in black families is the way in which husbands evaluate their wives' abilities. The next most influential factor is the husbands' income. Where wives are considered able and competent, black marriages are satisfactory to their members. In contrast, the strongest predictor of economic satisfaction in white families is the husband's income, and next is his education.

The third strongest relationship among the white women's data was a negative one—parenting. Women with children were less likely to be satisfied with their economic condition. There was no such relationship in the black data, suggesting again that children are valued, independent of economic conditions.

More highly educated black women are similar to white women in that husbands' income is a more significant influence. Next in importance is the way the wives' *own* abilities are perceived. These data suggest that the effects of husbands' income may be mediated by the wives' ability in black families and that their abilities may have a role in economic satisfaction that contributes to marital satisfaction.

Black and white husbands are more pleased with their economic conditions as the income they generate personally gets higher. Among black men, the next most significant influence was the wife's ability. In contrast, wife's ability was the *least* important influence among white men.

In considering overall the sources of economic satisfaction in black families, several issues emerge as significant. The ability of black wives, as perceived by themselves and by their husbands, contributes significantly to a sense of economic satisfaction in black families. Black women, understanding the barriers to black husband's income, find their own abilities even more important than their husbands' incomes. Black men, however, understanding the structure of sex roles in this society and the expectations of a man's capacity to support his family, are more satisfied if they themselves generate the income, and only then does it help to have a capable, task-oriented, and skillful wife.

Given such a source of potential conflict, how much understanding do black mates get from each other? How well do they feel they are in communication? Scanzoni attempted to see if "empathy" or satisfaction with communication was influenced by economic satisfaction, wife's employment, and such self-perceived personality characteristics as expressiveness of self-concept and authority.[82] Black women who worked full time felt less understood than others. All wives felt better understood when they were satisfied with their economic condition. Women who perceived themselves as expressive and women who felt they had authority also were satisfied with supportive relationships.

All men felt their wives communicated to them sufficiently and felt they were understood when they perceived their wives as capable. Wives' ability influenced the feeling that they were understood by all men. Families who communicated better were more satisfied with their use of leisure time, their companionship, and their sexual activity. Black and white men seemed to be equally satisfied with their leisure, companionship, and sex. Black women were less satisfied with these aspects of their lives.

The importance to all women of economic satisfaction in deriving the feeling that there is sufficient understanding and communication, which, in turn, affects their satisfaction with other areas of their lives, must be emphasized.

This importance of economic satisfaction must also be considered in light of the joint median incomes of black husbands and wives being less than the median income of just the husband in white families.

Further, it is significant that black women try to make up for this deficiency, and their contributions increase that median by a third. Consequently, they see their abilities as the next *important* source of marital satisfaction in that their abilities compensate for income deficiencies. Black husbands, on the other hand, give their *own* income resources priority. They want to make more money than their wives, as in the idealized American culture.

Although wives' abilities offset some of the effects of low income, empathy, communication, and understanding are affected by economic satisfaction. If husbands assign importance to their own income contributions, then, to the extent that this affects their economic satisfaction, they will be less satisfied with expressive relationships.

As evidenced from Scanzoni's study, the paths of influence from social status variables to marital satisfaction are many and complex. While the goal of most researchers has been to identify the causes of the high rates of marital instability among blacks, most research in this area has not focused on the dynamic processes that intervene between economic conditions and marital breakup. Counter to those simplistic studies that have related through speculation, low income, high female authority, and female employment to marital breakup, the Scanzoni data suggest that these variables may have interaction effects, and as such may either reinforce or disrupt marital solidarity.

There is a serious methodological flaw in much of this research literature, that is, the comparison of black levels of marital instability to white levels without trying to understand factors that influence the instability. Such comparisons have several underlying and highly questionable assumptions.

Given the differences in the structural constraints on black and white existence, can we assume that blacks and whites will respond in the same way to the same material? Or, is it possible that "pretty happy" for one group might mean the same thing as "very happy" for another? Ordinal scales, such as those measuring satisfaction, have no "zero point." That is, it is likely that there is no such thing as *zero* satisfaction. Do blacks and whites begin then at the same level?

Researchers who have attempted to elucidate the causal influences on marital satisfaction have found different variables to be meaningful to the racial groups. These variables are related to their history and experience. Therefore, wife's ability that has not been critical to white survival does not determine either *her* or *her husband's* economic satisfaction. On the other hand, "children," who have been a source of satisfaction to black families, as slaves and contemporaneously, do not depress the marital satisfaction of blacks as they do whites. Certainly differences in meaning indicate the need to develop empirically based research models that incorporate the "other" reality.

The most conclusive statement that can be based on the body of literature concerning black marital satisfaction is that black wives are less satisfied with their marriages than black husbands or white mates are with theirs. Concrete causes that have been indicated in the research are both structural and social-psychological. How these causes interact with family dynamics, processes, behavior, and events to create the variance in satisfaction is yet to be discerned. As suggested by the above studies, only with very complex research designs based on theory that incorporates a black reality will these causes be discerned.

NOTES

1. Moynihan, *The Negro Family.*

2. Frazier, *The Negro Family in the United States.*

3. See U.S. Department of Commerce, Bureau of the Census, *Money Income of Families and Persons in the United States: 1978.*

4. See U.S. Department of Commerce, *Marital Status and Living Arrangements: March 1979.*

5. Joseph Scott sees these pressures as causing a form of consensual polygamy in the black community. See "Black Polygamous Family Formation." *Alternative Lifestyles.* 3(1):41-63. 1980. Stewart also analyzes

this phenomenon, the existence of which he argues finds support in the recordings of Millie Jackson, a rhythm and blues recording artist. See John B. Stewart, "Perspectives on Black Families from Contemporary Soul Music—The Case of Millie Jackson." *Phylon.* 41(1):57-71. 1980.

6. See, especially, Oliver Cox, "Sex Ratio and Marital Status Among Negroes." *American Sociological Review.* 5:937-947. 1940; and Jacqueline J. Jackson, "But Where Are the Men?" *Black Scholar.* 3:30-41. 1977.

7. U.S. Department of Justice, Bureau of Justice Statistics, *Prisoners in State and Federal Institutions on December 31, 1978.* Washington, D.C., U.S. Government Printing Office. May 1980.

8. John Scanzoni, "Sex Roles, Economic Factors, and Marital Solidarity in Black and White Marriages." *Journal of Marriage and the Family.* 37:130-145. 1975.

9. Blood and Wolfe, *Husbands and Wives.*

10. Ibid.

11. Ibid.

12. The Moynihan propositions have been explored over and over within the context of the work of other researchers. For example, see Lee Rainwater, "Crucible of Identity: The Negro Lower-Class Family." *Daedalus.* 95:172-216. 1966. Also see Schulz, *Coming Up Black.*

13. William Brink and Louis Harris, eds. *Black and White.* New York: Simon and Schuster. 1967. Pages 268-269.

14. Russell Middleton and Snell Putney, "Dominance in Decisions in the Family: Race and Class Differences." *American Journal of Sociology.* 65:604-609. 1960.

15. Ibid.

16. Judith Hammond and J. Rex Enoch, "Conjugal Power Relations Among Black Working-Class Families." *Journal of Black Studies.* 7(1):107-123. 1976.

17. Kathryn Thomas Dietrich, "A Reexamination of the Myth of Black Matriarchy." *Journal of Marriage and the Family.* 37:367-374. 1975.

18. Vicky L. Cromwell and Ronald E. Cromwell, "Perceived Dominance in Decision Making and Conflict Resolution Among Anglo, Black and Chicano Couples." *Journal of Marriage and the Family.* 40(4):749-759. 1978.

19. Ibid.

20. Eleanor Engram, "Role Transition in Early Adulthood: Orientations of Young Black Women." In La Frances Rodgers-Rose, ed., *The Black Woman.* Beverly Hills, Calif.: Sage. 1980. Pages 175-187.

21. See U.S. Department of Commerce, Bureau of the Census, *American Families and Living Arrangements.* 1980.

22. *White House Conference on Families.* Volume 1, No. 10. August 1980.

Marriage 89

23. R. C. Hampton, "Husbands' Characteristics and Marital Disruption in Black Families." *Sociological Quarterly.* 20(2):255-266. 1979.

24. John H. Scanzoni, *The Black Family in Contemporary Society.* Boston: Allyn and Bacon. 1971.

25. Rainwater, "Some Aspects."

26. Joan Aldous, "Wives' Employment Status and Lower-Class Men as Husband-Fathers: Support for the Moynihan Thesis." *Journal of Marriage and the Family.* 31(8):469-476. 1969.

27. Ibid.

28. Ibid.

29. Ibid.

30. Ibid.

31. Nicholas Babchuk and John A. Ballweg, "Black Family Structure and Primary Relations." *Phylon.* 33(12):334-347. 1972.

32. S. Bould, "Black and White Families—Factors Affecting Wives' Contributions to Family Income Where Husbands' Income Is Low to Moderate." *Sociological Quarterly.* 18(4):536-547. 1977.

33. Noel A. Cazenave, "Middle Income Black Fathers—Analysis of the Provider Role." *Family Coordinator.* 28(4):583-593. 1979.

34. Hammond and Enoch, "Conjugal Power Relations Among Black Working-Class Families."

35. Charles L. McNair, "The Black Family is not a Matriarchal Family Form." *Negro Educational Review.* 26:93-100. 1975.

36. Engram, "Role Transition."

37. Willie Melton and Darwin L. Thomas. "Instrumental and Expressive Values in Mate Selection of Black and White College Students." *Journal of Marriage and the Family.* 38(3):509-517. 1976.

38. Leland J. Axelson, "The Working Wife: Differences in Perceptions Among Negro and White Males." *Journal of Marriage and the Family.* 32(8):457-465. 1970.

39. Melton and Thomas, "Instrumental and Expressive Values."

40. Joseph S. Himes, "Interrelation of Occupational and Spousal Roles in a Middle-Class Negro Neighborhood." *Marriage and Family Living.* 22:362-363. 1960.

41. Ibid.

42. Lois Meek Stolz, "Effects of Mothers' Employment on Children: Evidence from the Research." *Child Development.* 21:749-782. 1960.

43. Elizabeth Herzog and Cecelia E. Sudia, *Boys in Fatherless Families.* U.S. Department of Health, Education and Welfare, Office of Child Development, Children's Bureau. Washington, D.C.: U.S. Government Printing Office. 1970.

44. Bart Landry and Margaret Platt Jendrek, "Employment of Wives in Middle-Class Black Families." *Journal of Marriage and the Family.* 40(4):787-797. 1978.

45. Ibid.

46. Engram, "Role Transition."

47. Robert E. Riegel, *American Women.* Teaneck, N.J.: Farleigh Dickinson University Press. 1970.

48. See U.S. Department of Commerce, Bureau of the Census, *Money Income of Families and Persons in the United States: 1978.*

49. See, for example, Bonnie Thornton Dill, "The Dialectics of Black Womanhood: Towards a New Model of American Femininity." Unpublished Paper. Presented to the American Sociological Association. August, 1975.

50. Engram, "Role Transition."

51. See William Ryan, *Blaming The Victim.* Revised edition. New York: Vintage. 1976.

52. Moynihan, *The Negro Family.*

53. See Warren D. TenHouten. "The Black Family: Myth and Reality." *Psychiatry. 33:145-173. 1970.*

54. Lois W. Hoffman, "Mother's Enjoyment of Work and Effects on the Child." In F. Ivan Nye and Lois W. Hoffman, eds., *The Employed Mother in America.* Chicago: Rand McNally. 1963.

55. Ibid.

56. See Stolz, "Effects of Mothers' Employment."

57. See Eleanor Glueck and Sheldon Glueck, "Working Mothers and Delinquency." *Mental Hygiene.* 41:327-352. 1957.

58. Michael Schwartz, "Northern U.S. Negro Matriarchy: Status versus Authority." *Phylon.* 26:18-24. 1965.

59. Blood and Wolfe, *Husbands and Wives.*

60. Mirra Komarovsky, *Blue Collar Marriage.* New York: Random House. 1964.

61. Blood and Wolfe, *Husbands and Wives.*

62. Middleton and Putney, "Dominance in Decisions."

63. Schulz, *Coming Up Black.*

64. Schwartz, "Northern U.S. Negro Matriarchy."

65. Ibid.

66. Schulz, *Coming Up Black.*

67. Ladner, *Tomorrow's Tomorrow.*

68. Herbert H. Hyman and John Shelton Reed, "Black Matriarchy Reconsidered: Evidence from Secondary Analysis of Sample Surveys." *Public Opinion Quarterly.* 33:346-354. 1969.

69. Seymour Parker and Robert Kleiner, "Social and Psychological Dimensions of the Family Role Performance of the Negro Male." *Journal of Marriage and the Family.* 31:500-506. 1969.

70. Ibid.

71. Scanzoni, "Sex Roles, Economic Factors."

72. Cromwell and Cromwell, "Perceived Dominance in Decision Making."

73. Blood and Wolfe, *Husbands and Wives.*

74. Brink and Harris, *Black and White.*

75. Middleton and Putney, "Dominance in Decisions."

76. Aldous, "Wives' Employment Status."

77. Rainwater, "Some Aspects."

78. Karen S. Renne, "The Correlates of Dissatisfaction in Marriage." *Journal of Marriage and the Family.* 32:54-66. 1970.

79. Blood and Wolfe, *Husbands and Wives.*

80. Helena Z. Lopata, *Occupation Housewife.* New York: Oxford University Press. 1971.

81. Scanzoni, "Sex Roles, Economic Factors."

82. Ibid.

7

Child Rearing

This study does not undertake a review of that research in the sociology of education literature which links social structural and family structural variables to educational and occupational attainment. Instead, it focuses on what have been the major research topics in black family sociology pertaining to child-rearing practices and the development of identity and discusses the research that has been cited by other investigators in this area.

The theoretical system that has guided research in black child rearing and socialization is supported by the empirical realities that:

1. Black families with children are more likely than other families with children to be headed by the mother of the children. One-half of black children are born to unmarried women.
2. Black women, whether they head their families or share this responsibility with a husband or other person, are likely to be working full time. Contrary to popular opinion, they are unlikely to be on welfare.
    These data are used against black families as if black mother's work contributions were not the source of black survival.
3. Black children are studied to see if traditional sex-roles are favored.[1]

4. Black children are studied to see if little girls are "matriarchs" and little boys are "effeminate."[2]
5. Boys in fatherless homes[3] are studied for effeminacy and peer dependence.
6. Black fathers who are present are studied to see if they are more expressive than they should be, given the presumed dominance of women.[4]

Ryan terms this type of scientific "headhunting" the art of *Savage Discovery*. That is, discovering savages requires that those who wish to "blame the victims" of racism and discrimination for their own conditions must demonstrate that:

> The poor, the black, the ill, the jobless, the slum tenants, are different and strange. They must learn to conduct or interpret the research that shows how "these people" think in different patterns, cling to different values, seek different goals and learn different truths.[5]

Therefore, much of the research on black child rearing and socialization has been meant simply to show that there are differences.

Widely cited, early child-rearing literature suggests that there are few observable differences in the child-rearing behaviors of blacks and whites except behaviors related to weaning and toilet training. From comparisons of black and white mothers the classic study, conducted by Davis and Havighurst, concluded that black mothers are "more permissive" with respect to feeding and weaning, and white mothers are more permissive with respect to toilet training.[6] Just how these specific patterns affect future personality or behavior has not been discerned, neither was the relationship discussed within the context of the original study. This study, however, is often cited by other investigators to explain differences in black and white personality.

Radin and Kamii compare forty-five "culturally deprived" mothers to fifty "middle-class" white mothers of three-, four-, and five-year-olds living in a midwestern city.[7] The black sample was taken from a nursery school for "culturally disadvantaged children," and the white sample from a kindergarten in a middle-class neighborhood school. These researchers compared the Likert-type responses of these groups of mothers and found that the groups are similar with respect to the following views:

1. Children have rights as members of a family, and parents should earn their respect.
2. Children need discipline and firm rules.
3. Babies are helpless and need protection.

The racial groups expressed dissimilar views in their responses to the following:

1. Some children are just so bad that they must be taught to fear adults for their own good.
2. Children must not be encouraged to talk about their problems, as complaining will pester their mothers.

These dissimilarities did *not* reach statistical significance. In fact, the only significant difference between black and white mothers was in their responses to the statement, "Children should be protected from any disappointment, difficult situations, etc." Sixty-four percent of black mothers and only 12 percent of white mothers agreed with the statement. Black mothers more often agreed that:

1. Children should be taught to fear adults for their own good.
2. Children should not be encouraged to talk about their problems.
3. Sexual interests should be suppressed.
4. It is desirable to get children out of the helpless stage of infancy as soon as possible.[8]

In attitudes toward themselves, nuclear families, and society, the investigators found that black and white mothers agreed that husband and wife conflict is to be expected. Black mothers tended to see themselves as suffering, having little fun, and isolated from the rest of society, and believed that they should not find consolation outside of the home. Black mothers were significantly more likely to believe that it is the mother who is ultimately responsible for the welfare of the family.

The authors interpret the above findings as follows: "The picture thus emerges of a suffering matriarch who confines her life to her home, defines her own wisdom, feels no roots in society and eyes the outside world with great suspicion."[9] The investigators proceed to argue that low verbal ability among black school-age children is caused by matriarchal mothers who suppress verbal abilities with their overwhelming authority and dominance. Certainly, these conclusions have no empirical basis in this study.

First of all, the investigators have compared lower-class black mothers to middle-class white mothers, which almost ensures their "discovery" of differences.

Second, the authors are "defining the wisdom" and then asking the mothers to agree or disagree with them.

Third, the belief of the black mothers that they are ultimately responsible for the welfare of their children is no evidence of matriarchy, especially in light of the fact that 48 percent of the black women, compared to zero percent of the white women in the sample, headed their families, and probably, in reality, were ultimately responsible.

Fourth, since the researchers did not attempt to assess the verbal abilities of the children, they have no basis for saying that the authority patterns of their mothers had such an effect. This particular piece of research is exemplary of the posture that is often taken when researchers compare blacks to whites and highlights the need for research that is guided by some explicit theoretical formulation.

The same authors studied class differences in the socialization practices of black mothers. They hypothesized that lower-lower class and middle-class black mothers would be similar in child-rearing goals, but that "lower-lower" class mothers would interact with their children in such a manner as to "perpetuate a need for external controls."[10] This study compared twenty black mothers on public assistance to twenty whose husbands had "middle-class" occupations. The middle-class subjects were of a mean age five years older, had significantly more education, more fathers present, and fewer children than the lower-class subjects. The subjects were asked to separate eighteen cards containing child-rearing goals into three piles of six, representing "most important goals," "next most important goals," and "least important goals." Those cards in the "most important" category were assigned three points; those next in importance, two points; and the least important, one point. The scores of the lower- and middle-class groups were averaged for each goal, and tests were made for the significance of the difference between the means. The only differences among the eighteen goals were that lower-class mothers were more likely to value neatness and cleanliness, while the middle class valued "consideration for others," dependability, and that the "child should be liked by other adults."

While mothers were doing the card-sorting tasks, the authors observed their interaction with their children. Seventy-three percent of middle-class subjects met the child's need when it was expressed; they most often initiated interaction, communicated verbally, showed affection, and more often consulted with their children than lower-class mothers. Lower-class mothers more often made verbal requests in a demanding manner without explanation. There were no differences in negative reinforcement, but the middle-class mothers more often used positive reinforcement. The researchers conclude that positive reinforcement may result in anaclitic identification, that is, identification motivated by a fear of loss of love, rather than identification with an aggressor. Negative reinforcement, they argue, may be less effective in inhibiting impulses and may perpetuate the need for external controls. This negative reinforcement, they argue, may account for the lack of inner controls that may be observed among lower-class children in the school environment.

None of their interpretations finds empirical support in their study. While the investigators do show interaction to be different, the link between this interaction and external controls or identification is not established, and could not be with the particular design of the study. Thus, the conclusions are post hoc and speculative. They happen to coincide, however, with many of the prevailing myths regarding black families.

Assuming that socialization requirement are the same and that child-rearing literature provides valuable assistance to black and white parents, other researchers have compared parents' exposure to such literature.[11] Researchers find that black women at all education levels are less likely to be exposed to the literature than white women. The researchers interpret this lack of exposure, not as a choice black women make, but as the failure of a stationary black middle class to generate social pressure for assimilation.[12] The assumptions of comparability of black and white experiences has led many researchers to the hypothesis that differences in the lifestyles of blacks and whites may be attributed to class and not to color. Therefore, it is assumed that change is desirable in the direction of assimilation of white patterns, and it is hypothesized that economic mobility will effect change in that direction.

Blau compared the attitudes of black and white economically stationary and mobile mothers to see whether they, in raising their children, would like to be more restrictive, less restrictive, or the same, as their mothers were. Mobile white women were all inclined to change, whereas mobile black women were less inclined toward change than were black stationary women. The researcher attributes the differences to the absence of the middle-class model. This interpretation, of course, assumes that assimilation is desired and that middle-class black families have assimilated and, therefore, are models after which mobile families will pattern.

Because assimilation is the valued perspective and cultural patterns among black families have been ignored and, at best, misunderstood, child-rearing behaviors have been interpreted within Freudian psychoanalytic frameworks. The Freudians' overwhelming reliance on "the mother" as the source of external tension to the individual assumes a nonhostile external world. This assumption may not be valid in the world of black families.

In fact, these same studies have data that are left uninterpreted, but reflect the possibility that black women might socialize their children for the harsh realities of racism present in this society.

As we have seen, black mothers believe that children should be protected from disappointment and difficulty; for their own good they should be taught to fear adults; and it is desirable that children should be taught skills for independence as early as possible. Others who incorporate behavioral realities in the black experience find explanation of difference in these realities, rather than in theories of pathology that have fostered the stereotypes and myths. Young, in her anthropological studies of a southern black community, notes that black mothers raised their children in a "person-oriented," affectionate way. Babies, she said, from the time they are born, are held and passed from the arms and lap of one person to another. They are fondled and attended to constantly. Diapers are changed as soon as soiled, within the nurturing, loving context of the lap, where the baby spends so much time being loved and fondled. Toilet training, following this early nurturance, Young argues, is less stressful than coming after other methods of upbringing. Dougherty notes this also in her study of a rural Mississippi community.[13] Mothers in Dougherty's sample interacted extensively with their infants—touching, kissing, and holding the babies' hands to their mothers' bodies. The babies explored, in this way, the contours of the holders' faces and bodies.

Lewis observes that in families in her sample babies are held and fathers "mother" their children—with no indication of effeminacy or ineffectiveness—and mothers "father."[14] She argues that much of this behavior flows from an African orientation in which the tendency is to synthesize rather than to divide the world and where the emphasis is on personal characteristics as opposed to material and achievement of status.

Young[15] and Dougherty[16] also note the absence of material objects in the socialization of black infants. Lewis maintains that while these things are absent in early socialization, later socialization is structurally influenced to a much greater extent. It is there that the quest for material and status becomes salient.

It is clear that a significant proportion of black infants and children, if they make it,[17] make it within a context that is different from that of most white children.

Racism, poverty, and *an awareness of it* all come into play as black families socialize their children. Black children are taught that they are black and that this often means: cruel and unusual treatment,[18] they will have to be twice as good if they wish to succeed,[19] and they must view the environment as hostile.[20] These admonitions have often been interpreted as "black paranoia," although in such an environment, not to be paranoid may be unhealthy.

Contemporary researchers have noted that young blacks from different families who have not been socialized in this way and who take "economic survival" for granted are ill-prepared for the racism they encounter. It is theorized that the increasingly disproportionate rate of suicide among young black men and women manifests their lack of survival skills.[21] This is an area in which there is a demonstrated need for research.

Overwhelmingly, the literature on child-rearing practices presents empirical evidence that there are black/white differences in patterns of child rearing. Whether these differences are derived from uncontrolled structural forces, including socio-economic status and racism, have behavioral correlates, or cause certain outcomes in the personality or behavior, or both dimensions, of black and white children has not been sub-stantiated. These are, however, several of the questions regarding early childhood socialization which, if answered, would aid in the development of successful models of parenting.

Consistent with stereotypes of black adult role reversal, much of the child-rearing literature is given over to the discussion of processes of identification. Concern that black pathology is the result of character disorder, led Dai to conclude from case studies of delinquent and emotionally troubled black children that personality problems of black children result from interpersonal relationships with the family, matriarchy, and broken homes.[22] Although cited in more recent literature, it appears that this primary work was based on an obscure number of case studies.

Believing that black adolescent males are less masculine than they should be, Hetherington attempted to assess the effects of race, father absence, and time of the father's departure on their sex-typed behavior.[23] The sample included thirty-two black and thirty-two white first-born boys between the ages of nine and twelve who attended a recreation center in a lower-class urban area. Sixteen in each racial group were in father-absent homes, and eight of these sixteen had fathers who left when the boys were four years old or younger, while the other eight had fathers who left after they were six years old. There were no father substitutes in these homes.

A male recreation director was asked to rate the following attributes of the subjects on a seven point scale: (1) dependency on adults, (2) dependency on peers, (3) independence, (4) aggression, (5) ability in physical activities. The data indicated that father-absent boys were more dependent on peers than father-present boys. Father-present boys, and those whose fathers left after they were six years old, were more aggressive than the others. Father-present boys and boys whose fathers left later had more masculine role preference as measured by the "IT" scale.[24] The "IT" scale for children, developed by Brown, asked the subject (1) to state his preferences for eight toys from among sixteen, eight of which are considered masculine and eight feminine; (2) to state which he'd rather be of eight male/female alternatives, for example, Indian chief or Indian princess; and (3) to state which one of four child-figures he'd rather be, boyish girl, girlish boy, boy, or girl. Boys from early separated families played fewer physical games involving contact, but black, early-separated boys played significantly more of these games than white boys with the same family status. While the author concludes that there are no racial differences in the recreation center, she goes on to say that "boys who lost their fathers early, before identification can be assumed to have been completed, showed considerable deviation in sex-typed traits."[25]

It is astonishing that such a conclusion should be based on a study employing this type of methodology. First of all, the nonrandom selection of boys from the recreation center might have contained father-present boys who were significantly above the population mean on sex-typed traits. Second, there was no analysis done of family size or sex of sibling, both of which might influence these traits. Third, the method has a high potential for response bias, since it relied solely on the subjective evaluation of the recreation director. This study is cited again and again as evidence of the internalization of pathological male roles.

Biller looked at the effects of father absence on the "masculine development" of lower-class black and white boys.[26] His sample included fifteen black and fourteen white Durham, North Carolina, boys who were participating in an educational improvement project. The boys in the sample ranged in age from five years ten months to six years eleven months; all were of low socio-economic status and had an equivalent sibling distribution. There were six black and five white boys with fathers who were absent at least two years. Sex role identification was assessed by the "IT" test, and teachers were asked to rate "overt masculinity." Their data indicate more masculine "IT" scores among father-present boys than among father-absent boys, but no differences in overt masculinity ratings. The investigators found that blacks had lower "IT" scores. No racial differences in overt masculinity were apparent. A two-way analysis of variance of "IT" scores with race and father availability factor to be significant at the .025 level of statistical significance; race was significant at the .05 level, and there were no interaction effects. Both white, father-present and father-absent boys had higher "IT" scores than black boys with the same family status.

The author concludes that young boys seem to have even more difficulty in developing masculine self-concepts in families in which fathers are absent or ineffectual and in which little value is attached to being a male, and being masculine. It appears that a vague or feminine orientation may persist even though a boy becomes masculine in other aspects of his behavior. He further argues that the reason blacks, although quite unmasculine in sex role orientation, act quite masculine in overt behavior is that their overt masculinity is "compensatory reaction against sex role conflict."

Such conclusions are certainly not valid, inasmuch as the investigator did not measure "father ineffectuality," "valuation of maleness and/or masculinity," or "masculine self-concepts." Although he says that black boys are feminine in orientation based on the "IT" scale scores, he does not present supportive data; therefore, the reader cannot discern whether scores were actually feminine or simply less masculine than white boys' scores. How masculine is "masculine" anyway? Again, the use of ordinal data is questionable. Is there a point of zero masculinity? Finally, the attribution of overt masculinity to a psychological defense mechanism is entirely unfounded and has all the appearances of being a desperate post hoc attempt to salvage a thesis. Again, the subjects encounter the "damned-if-you-do, damned-if-you-don't" posture of scientific racism.

Barclay and Cusumano investigated the effects of father absence and "cross-sex identity" on field dependent[27] behavior with a sample of forty male adolescents.[28] An experimental group of ten father-absent black and ten father-absent white males was compared to ten father-present boys from each racial group. Controls were matched to experimentals on age, grade-point average, Intelligence Quotient (I.Q.), and socio-economic status. Overt sex role identification was measured by Gough's femininity scale.[29] Cross-sex or same-sex identity was measured by the adolescents' ratings of themselves and their parents on a series of bipolar adjectives, such as active-passive and rugged-delicate. The degree of father or mother similarity was taken as a measure of their same or cross-sex identity.

The investigators argue that theoretically, the more field dependent a subject is, the greater is his identification with the "passive maternal model." The investigators present no evidence supporting this theory or linking field dependence to passivity or "feminine" characteristics. Black subjects had a higher mean field dependence score (7.58) than white subjects (5.68). "Father-present" boys had lower means than "father-absent" boys. The researchers do not report whether these differences are statistically significant. There were no differences between "racial" or father availability groups on the Gough or on the semantic differential test. As in the Biller study,[30] these researchers interpret their findings to indicate that blacks and father-absent boys, while *overtly masculine*, have an underlying feminine identification. Their overt masculinity, they argue, is a defensive reaction—compensatory masculinity. Why then aren't father-absent boys more overtly masculine than father-present boys? These researchers argue, without a basis, that father-absent boys would have begun at lower levels of overt masculinity and thus, would have gone further to reach those levels.

While the processes described above are potentially true, they are not borne out by the research. There is no evidence that father-absent boys begin at different levels of overt masculinity, and there is no evidence that field dependence measures underlying feminine orientations. The attribution of overt masculine behavior to a psychological defense mechanism for one group of boys and to normal behavior for the other reflects the "damned-if-you-do, damned-if-you-don't" interpretive framework which, I have argued, is often brought to bear on those groups in society who do not mirror and are denied middle-class styles of life.

Stephens surveyed thirty-seven social workers who were each asked to name five mother-child families in which there was a ten-year-old son and in which there were "usually no men present" during the first six years of the son's life.[31] They were also asked to name mother-father families with mothers and fathers present and with a ten-year-old son. Social workers then matched families without fathers with two-parent families on class, ethnicity, and "completeness of their knowledge of them and their family histories." Social workers then listed their own answers to the following questions, based on their knowledge of the families' homes:

1. Does the boy belong to a delinquent group now, or in the past?
2. Which boy appears more anxious about sex?
3. Which boy is most effeminate?
4. Which boy shows greatest hostility toward other men?
5. Which mother is most jealous of her son's girlfriends?
6. Which mother has the most negative attitude toward men?

Of course, the investigators conclude from their data, that father-absent boys are more likely to be delinquent, more ambivalent about sex, more effeminate, and hostile toward men. However, the phrasing, the questions, and the conduct of the study permits so much bias as to make the conclusions of little worth. Not only were the questions written so as to force social workers to attribute a deviant characteristic to one or the other of her subjects, but also the social workers themselves represent a "deviant" group, since they were all attendant at a conference on "mothers without husbands."

Although Cavan is often cited in support of the thesis of the detrimental effect of black families on children, her study is a purely impressionistic rehashing of E. Franklin Frazier's study of the Negro family in Chicago.[32] Cavan presents a table from the Frazier work showing an inverse relationship between such attributes as class, illegitimacy, delinquency, and female-headed families to launch a discussion regarding the effects of matriarchy, and all the other stereotyped pathologies, on identification and delinquency.

Rubin expected fatherless black boys to have lower self-esteem than white boys.[33] He didn't find this to be the case and suggests that they find role models "in the street." Since he finds no differences in fathered and fatherless boys, he suggests that present fathers are demoralized.

Iscoe, Williams, and Harvey attribute differences in conformity patterns among black and white seven-, nine-, twelve-, and fifteen-year-old males and females to differences in conformity patterns among family role structures.[34] The sample, which includes sixty-four males and sixty-four females of each race, was selected from segregated urban public schools. Fifty percent of the white sample were middle class and the rest upper-lower class. The total black sample was lower class and had higher proportions of absent fathers and working mothers. Subjects were requested to count metronome clicks, first in an "alone" condition, and again when they were hearing voices that they construed to be other subjects undergoing the same experiment. Two criterion scores were taken: (1) errors made in the "alone" condition, and (2) errors made while listening to the voices of subjects presumed to be taking the test. Then, a comparison of these scores was made in relation to sex, age, race, and I.Q., and all second order interactions.

Sex, race, and I.Q. alone had no effect on conformity, but there was a significant sex-times-race interaction. While black and white males were similar in conformity, black females were much less conforming than all males and white females. There was an inverse relationship between age and conformity and an age-times-race interaction. Among white subjects, conformity increased up to age twelve, then decreased by age fifteen. Conformity decreased among blacks after nine years. An I.Q.-times-race interaction revealed that black subjects below 80 I.Q. conformed much less than whites at that level and that above 80 in I.Q. subjects of both races decreased in conformity behavior. While the researchers just as well might have interpreted the age-times-race effect as being contradictory to the theses regarding peer dependence of black youth, this finding was passed over. Rather, they focused on the race-sex interaction. The investigators argue that the nonconformity of black females is the result of the matriarchal social structure of which she is a member, and, they argue, it reflects the fact that, historically, black females have been able to "get away with more" than black males. The interpretation ignores the finding that black females are also less conforming than white males and females; and it is a very dubious interpretation to say that black females have historically "gotten away with more" than these two groups. In addition, no measures were taken in this study for the linking of matriarchy to conformity patterns. This methodology is another example of research in which the investigators have sorted through their findings to select those that validate some covert assumptions about the deviance inherent in black family processes and have ignored those findings that may invalidate such notions.

Aldous attempted to see if father-absence influenced four year olds' perceptions of male and female adult roles across races and classes. In this comparison of father-absent to father-present children, the investigator found that all children tended to see fathers as taking the traditional breadwinner role.

She concludes that children are not dependent on parental sources for sex role information. Several other researchers have confirmed this finding.[35]

Because the researcher also subscribes to themes of the pathology of the black male adult and did not expect negative results, she went on to speculate as to why there is adult "mental instability" in this group. She argues the "roots of mental instability may be in the realization that he failed to meet those expectations he's had since an early age."

Baughman and Dahlstrom found from extensive interviews with ninety black and white children and their mothers that both racial groups perceived their fathers to be dominant in the home, black family members perceived their husbands and fathers as subordinate and with little authority in the community.[36] They suggest that this external deprecation may enter familial relationships, although they did not find evidence of it, and, in any case, their design did not test for such a relationship.

Karl King studied perceptions of familial power structures held by 226 black males and 313 black females, aged fourteen.[37] The sample was asked whether one or both parents were likely to make decisions regarding television programs, large purchases, child punishment, adolescent job allocation, and adolescent restriction. King's sample overwhelmingly viewed power as sex related, across occupational levels of their parents. Males tended to view their fathers as more autonomous, and females their mothers as more autonomous. These data suggest that rather than identifying with "cross-sex" roles, the models, as the adolescent perceives them, are consistent with the culturally valued ones.

Frumkin also noted a preference for egalitarian role structures among forty black college students.[38] These students rated egalitarian organization, as opposed to male or female dominant organization, as generally desirable and as desired by themselves.

Lystad studied intergenerational patterns of family roles, achievements, and aspirations among one hundred urban New Orleans black families.[39] A random sample of subjects was taken from admission records of a prenatal clinic which handles 90 percent of the black births in that area. Fifty-two of the respondents had lived in two-parent families until age sixteen. Fifteen had lost a parent due to death prior to age sixteen, and thirty-five came from one-parent families created by illegitimacy, separation, or divorce.

She found no significant intergenerational differences between these rates, but the researchers did not attempt to correlate family types across individuals. They found that there was little intergenerational change in perceived roles of mothers and fathers based on the subjects' reports of these roles in both their families of orientation and procreation. It was also found that, without respect to social class, mothers all desired more education for their children than they themselves had. They found significant downward mobility between these respondents and their parents; this may, however, be a function of the respondent's stage in the family life cycle, that is, parents' reported occupations may have been from a later "family life cycle" stage. On the other hand, it may reflect the inability of black parents of middle-class status to "place" their offspring in that same status as happens in the white community.

Smith and Abrahamson in a study of the correlates of mobility aspirations matched thirty-three black and thirty-three white adolescents on age, sex, intelligence, and social status variables.[40] They found that family experiences, as defined, were not related to achievement and mobility aspirations, but there was a slight tendency for those adolescents who felt unwanted by their mothers to have higher aspirations. The only differences between black and white adolescents were that blacks found the success goals of money and prestige more important, while whites viewed happiness as more important. There were no racial differences in the adolescents' reactions to family discipline, perceptions of family attitudes toward them, punishment, reactions to school grades, tendency to seek advice from parents, evaluations of fathers' success, or perceptions of how well their families get along with each other.

The author concludes the study by saying that perhaps the racial groups are becoming psychologically less differentiated as they become more socially integrated. Yet, there was never empirical evidence that they were ever psychologically apart.

Again, this study bespeaks the tendency of social researchers to invoke all the stereotypes and gloss over or explain away their negative results.

Similarly, researchers have approached the study of self-esteem among black youth with the assumption that black youth feel inadequate as a consequence of not having fathers.[41] One such study that expected lower self-esteem among fatherless boys did not find it and explained the findings as follows:

1. Fatherless boys may find role models in the streets, thus elevating their concepts.
2. Those with fathers probably have demoralized fathers thus depressing their self-esteem.[42]

The researcher does not say whether self-concept measures are high, low, positive, or negative. Efforts are focused on explaining away negative results. Again the stereotypes are salvaged, and black youth are "damned-if-they-do, damned-if-they-don't."

Research on the effects of father absence has been flawed by unclear definitions of father absence, by the incorporation of military, incarcerated, and temporary absences into the same data and by analyses that rest on more permanent absences such as divorce, widowhood, and marriage separation. Surely there are socially desirable forms of father absence. However, statistics like these have been used extensively in portrayals of the black family as pathologically disrupted.[43]

Father absence cannot be measured by marital status of mothers anyway, since the quantity and quality of paternal interaction in divorced and separated families can easily be superior to that of intact families. Fathers in many intact families rarely see their children during the work week, and, in many cases, their interaction may be characterized as cold and distant. Earl noted in her study of fifty-three black, male children, between seven and twelve years of age that eight saw their biological fathers daily, fifteen once a week, and four at least twice a month.[44] Only eleven sons had no contact with their fathers. However, all of the boys saw other male relatives often: 44 percent saw uncles once a week or more often; 20 percent saw their grandfathers once a week or more often; 77 percent saw a male cousin at least once weekly, and of these, 52 percent saw a cousin daily; and 15 percent saw an older brother daily. In addition, 76 percent of the mothers in the sample had boyfriends whom they reported their sons seeing three or four times weekly, and 84 percent of the boys identified a neighborhood man as a friend.[45]

A pathology of male absence cannot, therefore, be assumed on the basis of marital status. Whether male absence is pathological at all is moot, since young males with absolutely no adult male presence have yet to be studied by social science researchers.

Probably because identification is a psychological process, researchers in this area have been more unrestrained when attributing pathology to blacks as they observe black-white differences. But deserving of even *more* criticism are the tendencies of the same researchers to seek explanations with which they can also interpret black-white *similarities* as being evidence of the *same* pathologies.

The foregoing assessment of the research literature regarding sex-role identity—literature that is often cited in discussions of the black family —finds that the major conclusions, although widely cited, often are not derived from the empirical findings and often may be questioned on both empirical and logical grounds. In some cases data are contrived to fit the stereotypes. That the phenomenon researchers variously term sex-role identity, orientation, or preference, has other than an imagined impact on adult family behavior or personality is an even less substantiated thesis that is, as yet, without an empirical basis.

NOTES

1. Karl King, Thomas J. Abernathy, and Ann H. Chapman, "Black Adolescents' Views of Maternal Employment as a Threat to the Marital Relationship: 1963-1973." *Journal of Marriage and the Family*. 38(4):733-737. 1976.

2. E. Mavis Hetherington, "Effects of Paternal Absence on Sex-Typed Behaviors in Negro and White Pre-Adolescent Males." *Journal of Personality and Social Psychology*. 4:87-91. 1966.

3. Roger Harvey Rubin, *Matricentric Family Structure and the Self-Attitudes of Negro Children.* San Francisco: R & E Publishing Co. 1976.

4. Sharon Pricebonham and P. Skeen, "Comparison of Black and White Fathers With Implications for Parent Education. *Family Coordinator.* 28(10):53-59. 1979.

5. Ryan, *Blaming the Victim.* Page 10.

6. Allison Davis and Robert J. Havighurst, "Social Class and Color Differences in Child Rearing." *American Sociological Review.* 11:698-710. 1946.

7. Norma Radin and Constance K. Kamii, "The Child Rearing Attitudes of Disadvantaged Negro Mothers and Some Educational Implications." *Journal of Negro Education.* 34:138-146. 1965.

8. Ibid.

9. Ibid.

10. Constance K. Kamii and Norma Radin, "Class Differences in the Socialization Practices of Negro Mothers." *Journal of Marriage and the Family.* 29:302-310. 1967.

11. Zena Smith Blau, "Exposure to Child-Rearing Experts: A Structural Interpretation of Class-Color Differences." *American Journal of Sociology.* 69:596-608. 1964.

12. Ibid.

13. See Virginia Heyer Young, "Family and Childhood in a Southern Negro Community." *American Anthropologist.* 72(2):269-288. 1970; and Molly Dougherty, *Becoming a Woman in Rural Black Culture.* Nashville, Tenn.: Vanderbilt University Press. 1978.

14. Diane K. Lewis, "Black Family: Socialization and Sex Roles." *Phylon* 36:221-237. 1975.

15. See Young, "Family and Childhood."

16. Dougherty, *Becoming a Woman.*

17. Lewis, "Black Family: Socialization."

18. Nobles, *Formulative and Empirical Study.*

19. Scanzoni, *Black Families in Contemporary Society.*

20. Nobles, *Formulative and Empirical Study.*

21. Alvin Poussaint notes the differential suicide rates between black Africans who have a sense of group belonging and black North Americans who increasingly have developed a sense of individuality. Black male youth have rising rates of suicide. See, "Rising Suicide Rates Among Blacks." *Urban League Review.* 3(1):22-30. 1977.

22. B. Dai, "Some Problems of Personality Development Among Negro Children." In C. Kluckholn, H. A. Murray, and D. M. Schneider, eds. *Personality in Nature, Society and Culture.* New York: Knopf. 1953. Pages 545-566.

23. Hetherington. "Effects of Paternal Absence."

24. Ibid.

25. Ibid.

26. Biller, "A Note on Father Absence."

27. The field dependency test measures the degree to which the subject is perceptually dependent on a surrounding frame when asked to tilt a rod within the frame to a vertical position. If the subject adjusts the rod toward the angle of its surrounding frame, his perception is characterized as being "field dependent."

28. A. G. Barclay and D. Cusumano, "Father Absence, Cross-Sex Identity and Field Dependent Behavior in Male Adolescents." *Child Development.* 38(3):243-250. 1967.

29. Ibid.

30. Biller, "A Note on Father Absence."

31. William N. Stephens, "Judgement by Social Workers on Boys and Mothers in Fatherless Families." *Journal of Genetic Psychology.* 99:59-64. 1961.

32. Ruth Shonle Cavan, "Negro Family Disorganization and Juvenile Delinquency." *Journal of Negro Education.* 28:230-239. 1959.

33. Rubin, *Matricentric Family Structure.*

34. Ira Iscoe, Martha Williams, and Jerry Harvey, "Age, Intelligence, and Sex as Variables in the Conformity Behavior of Negro and White Children." *Child Development.* 35:451-460. 1964.

35. Charles B. Wilkinson and William A. O'Connor, "Growing Up Male in a Black Single-Parent Family." *Psychiatric Annals.* 7(7):50-51, 55-59. 1977.

36. E. Earl Baughman and W. G. Dahlstrom, *Negro and White Children: A Psychological Study in the Rural South.* New York: Academic Press. 1968.

37. Karl King, "Adolescent Perception of Power Structure in the Negro Family." *Journal of Marriage and the Family.* 31:751-755. 1969.

38. Frumkin, "Attitudes of Negro College Students Toward Intrafamily Leadership and Control."

39. M. H. Lystad, "Family Patterns, Achievements and Aspirations of Urban Negroes." *Sociology and Social Research.* 45:281-288. 1961.

40. Howard P. Smith and Marcia Abrahamson, "Racial and Family Experience Correlates of Mobility Aspirations." *Journal of Negro Education.* 31:117-124. 1962.

41. Rubin, *Matricentric Family Structure.*

42. Ibid.

43. See Herzog and Sudia, *Boys in Fatherless Families.*

44. Earl and Lohmann, "Absent Fathers."

45. Ibid.

8

Marital Disruption

It is fair to say that, to some extent, much of the research of the past quarter century that has examined black families in American society has been undertaken in response to rising rates of divorce and separation. Consistent with that concern is the very serious implication that black families experiencing such dislocation and disorganization may be inadequate socializing agents for the future of black society. It is the assumption of such inadequacy that has fostered social and economic policies that are biased against the strengths of black families.[1]

By employing rates of divorce and separation as indicators, researchers can easily document that black Americans have relatively higher rates of marital instability than white Americans (see table 8.1).[2] Whether the causes of such instability lie in the larger social structure or in a black subculture has been a major issue of debate in the black family literature.[3]

TABLE 8.1   Divorced Persons per One Thousand
Married Persons, Black and White

	White	Black
1979	84	197
1975	64	136
1970	44	83
1960	35	62

Source: Adapted from U.S. Department of Commerce, Bureau of the Census, *Marital Status and Living Arrangements: March, 1979.*

Moynihan, in an analysis of census data, demonstrated an aggregate relationship between fluctuations in the unemployment rates of black males, marital disruption of blacks, rates of female-headed households, and illegitimacy in the same communities.[4] He attributed these rates to a cultural pathology. The data were *aggregate* and, although suggestive of individual relationships, cannot be used to determine whether the families of the unemployed were the ones that broke up, had illegitimate children, had children who dropped out of school, or had children who failed armed forces exams. Yet, these are the interpretations that were given to the data.

Pursuing this same line of analysis with 1960 census data, Udry found that when status is measured by education level, the relationship between status and marital disruption is negative for both blacks and whites of both sexes.[5] That is, the more highly educated people were most likely to be in intact families. When status was measured by occupation, Udry found an inverse relationship to exist for men, but not for women, of both races. That is, women's occupations did not influence their marital status. Black marriages were observed to be more unstable than white marriages across occupational and educational levels. Udry's data suggest that education is an important source of marital solidarity for both races, while the man's occupation is critical for his marriage. The higher rates of disruption among blacks without respect to the socio-economic differences cannot be interpreted as racial effects, however, since such other socio-economic indices such as income may explain the variance. In fact, income may be grossly unequal across educational and occupational levels when comparing blacks to whites.

In a later study, Udry analyzed the same data for the effects of income on marital stability.[6] He found a positive relationship between income and marital stability for both races. As income increased, however, the ratio of nonwhite to white instability increased. While Udry maintains that the data suggest that more than socio-economic differences are operating, it appears he does so only because social scientists have defined and measured socio-economic status so narrowly. Other possible explanatory factors may be differences in fertility, number of contributors to family income, and such various discriminatory experiences as differences in value received for the same expenditure.

Bernard studied marital stability within a sample of husbands from husband-wife families, in 89.8 percent of which it was the wife's first marriage.[7] The investigator selected marriages with husbands aged forty-five to fifty-four in order to minimize the probability of future marital disruption. She matched racial groups on education, income, and occupation and found that fewer black husbands were likely to have been married only once despite their status. She argues that the greater marital instability of black males must be the result of social-psychological or cultural factors. According to Bernard, "externally adaptive" and "acculturated" black families exist dually at all levels of black society, so that higher rates of "instability" can be found at all levels. She maintains that instability in the high socio-economic status level would be attributable to either externally adapted blacks among that group or to the acculturated, socially mobile who are suffering from "status striving" stress.

Again, we see a theory that dooms black families to pathology whether they do or do not mirror the dominant societal pattern. These interpretations are, of course, post hoc, without empirical basis; yet this work, as others have been, is widely cited as proffering supportive data.[8]

Schermerhorn criticizes Bernard's conclusions on the basis that the individuals in her sample were born between the years 1906 and 1915, years of the great migration, and, thus, would have been comparable to other first-generation *immigrant* groups to whom we do not extend such classifications.[9] Rainwater comments that Bernard might have reduced the variance in instability by entering variables to account for geographic mobility, social mobility, fertility, and adjustments for differential occupations and education.[10]

Chilman's commentary is also critical of the age group Bernard selected, since, she argues, the child-bearing years are theoretically more important.[11] She adds as another criticism that housing, intimidation, and other factors that militate against family stability also warrant inclusion in such studies. In his analysis of case workers concerned with interstate petitions for nonsupport, Monahan reviewed all of the cases initiated in the Philadelphia Domestic Relations Court in a one-year period.[12] He found that black and white cases differed with respect to age at marriage, fertility, premarital pregnancies, region of birth, region of marriage, and husband's occupation. The mean age of marriage for blacks in their caseloads was lower, fertility and premarital pregnancy rates were higher, and the duration of marriage was shorter. Sixty-five percent of the whites were born in Philadelphia, and 81 percent of the blacks were born in the South. Sixty-six percent of the blacks were married in the South, while 90 percent of the whites were married in Philadelphia. None of the blacks had white-collar occupations, but thirty percent of the whites did. This study highlights the complexity of the issues surrounding differential marital stability rates. Such studies encompass many variables that, although they may not pertain directly to socio-economic status, have a profound impact on general economic conditions and, therefore, an impact on the occupations and incomes of men. Men, as discerned in the research above (see Chapter 5), designate their own incomes and occupations as the most important influences on their marital satisfaction.

Miao[13] argues that while Moynihan[14] drew attention to differential rates of marital instability of blacks, he did not note whether the rates for whites were also sensitive to fluctuations in unemployment. When indexing marital instability as separation rates or as separation and divorce rates, she observed that during the 1950s the white pattern mirrored the nonwhite pattern. But after this period, white rates continued to increase, as they did for blacks, insensitive to employment patterns. Rather than attributing these increases to self-perpetuated pathology, as Moynihan has argued, Miao argues that other social factors may either have a depressing or stimulating effect on marital disruption rates. For example, she argues that a decreased rate of disruption among blacks during the period 1967 to 1968, in spite of high unemployment, may be due to the social cohesion stimulated by the urban riots. Increases may be due to more liberalized ideologies that encourage *unhappy* couples to part, and perhaps more liberalized welfare laws make such separations tenable alternatives. There is considerable evidence that happy, communicative family environments, whether of intact or broken marriages, are healthier milieux for the growth and development of their members than are those in which the spouses merely stay together or stay together in conflict.

To investigate and test theses of the intergenerational effects of marital stability, Duncan and Duncan looked at the relationship between family of orientation structure and occupational success among men in families of procreation with their spouses present.[15] They argue that difference in success is attributable to differences in the orientation family structure. They found slightly higher occupational levels among men with intact family backgrounds and greater social mobility. The relationship was more pronounced for blacks. The investigators analyzed socio-economic status in terms of "age at first marriage," "full-time occupation," "socio-economic status score of job," and "grade of school completed upon taking first job." They found that education had the highest explanatory power, that is, men with more education had better jobs. Men from intact families had translated education into higher occupational achievement, although entry into the occupational arena may have been at equal levels for men of both groups. There was no measure of training undertaken after the first job, and little information was gathered from which one could theorize as to what there is about an intact family that creates such differences. Duncan and Duncan also note that the influence in female-headed black families does not come from the status of the woman's job, but from the *regularity* of her work-force attachment; in white female-headed families, however, both are said to have an effect.

Black men with equal education from intact families were on the average of nineteen points lower on the occupational scale than white men with the same educational and family background. This discrepancy demonstrates that black and white males are not rewarded equally for adherence to socially prescribed traditions. Rather than demonstrating subculturally stabilized pathology among black Americans, it demonstrates the stabilization of discriminatory forces in the larger society.

Herzog argues that the position one takes as to whether black family instability is attributable to poverty, cultural inheritance, or a cycle of self-perpetuating pathology is critical, since the theory of its cause implies its solution.[16] While some researchers believe that it is time to subordinate social, economic, and legal status reform to interventionary and remedial policies directed toward black family stability, the necessity for doing so is not indicated by the extant research. Rather than developing policies to remedy the stereotypical and undocumented pathology in black families, policymakers should consider interventions that would break the cycles of structural denial of earned rewards. To what extent are these myths structured into the planning of services for and policies to affect black families? And being believed, do the myths become self-fulfilling prophecies?

Willie and Weinandy studied the structure and composition of "stable" and "problem" families identified by a housing project supervisor.[17] They found that 50 percent of the families described as problems had disintegrated after moving into the housing project. This finding suggests that (1) poverty may have been a primary cause of marital breakup, and (2) neighborhood conditions may have an independent effect on marital stability. The researchers maintain that housing project conditions foster an absence of control and commitment to *values* [my emphasis], which themselves may be causal variables. The Willie and Weinandy study, although suggestive of other explanations of marital disruption, is methodologically too unsound to stimulate generalization. The data were based on the housing director's impressions as he was asked to distinguish "problem" from "stable" families. It does, however, imply a serious need for careful research in this area.

Similar hypotheses are suggested by Rainwater's analysis of case studies from lower-class housing project residents in Saint Louis, but he does not perceive them.[18] Rainwater maintains that the ghetto comprises an adaptive subculture that rewards behavior and attitudes that are antithetical to the values of the larger society. While certain postures may be functional for survival within such a subculture, they may, he maintains, be malfunctional for success within the broader community. Again it is suggested that we blacks are "damned-if-we-do, damned-if-we-don't." It is implied that if we survive we will not be successful. In any case, if Rainwater is correct, his thesis raises questions regarding the societal role in maintaining conditions that doom black children from birth.

Bernard also argues that because neighborhoods are racially segregated, "externally adapted" and "acculturated" black families must live side by side to the detriment of the acculturated group.[19] She argues that externally adapted families are defined as "lowlifes" in the black community, and that these coexist with the "respectables" at each socio-economic status level. The ethos of the externally adapted culture, she maintains, is hedonistic and pleasure loving, while the acculturated value "delayed gratification," as do members of the white middle class whom they are trying to approximate.[20] On the one hand, Bernard is liberal in her discussion, as she is at least sensitive to variations within the black community, unlike most researchers who treat blacks as a monolith. On the other hand, her assumption that the goal of black families should be to be "respectable" by approximating the white middle class is a matter of debate. There is something of value to be found in black communities, something that is respectable, that is pleasure loving, and that is not white middle-class. Bernard's interpretations of what she sees are thus rooted in a conservative bias. White neighborhoods are also racially segregated. It is unlikely that the author would see whites' living side by side as problematic. Such a scientific perspective on black America is divisive. It precludes the facts that most blacks have poor relatives and country cousins and that all have something of value to share.

Hannerz also notes variation in his ethnographic account of a Washington, D.C., ghetto group.[21] He argues that within the neighborhood he studied there were four distinct categories of people: mainstreamers, street families, swingers, and the street corner man. He describes the mainstreamers as those who are seen by the community as respectable and stable. Theirs are mostly two-parent households, headed by blue-collar workers with stable employment, who mirror the dominant culture in values and aspirations for themselves and their children. Street families, he argues, can be recognized by their lifestyle, that is, as the weather permits, these families are seen to be sharing conversation on their own or a neighbor's stoop, while children are playing up and down the street. The most typical of these units, he argues, is a household headed by a woman and often shared by other mothers and their children, grandmothers, or siblings, or any combination of these people. To the observer the most distinctive feature of these household groups, Hannerz maintains, is the number of children and the ease with which a broad spectrum of persons can be seen to flow in and out of these families. Swingers are so named by the researcher because of their "gay, carefree lifestyle." According to Hannerz, this group is usually made up of young adults who emphasize natty clothing, partying, and "clean" or fashionable cars. Although both sexes make up this group, females are usually more temporary members as they often drop out to have children, establish more permanent conjugal bonds, or are forced by parents to stay at home to tend to their own offspring. Hannerz says that the hedonistic lifestyle, along with the unstable employment of males in this group, causes males to establish as fragile bonds and transient relationships as possible.[22]

Street corner men in contrast to swingers are usually older and more residentially stable within the community. Usually beset by long periods of unemployment, these men spend time with each other "drinking wine" on street corners, laughing, and telling jokes. Hannerz maintains these men usually have ties with the women in street families and father some of their children. He concludes from his analysis of these diverse styles that there are some behaviors that are adaptive for the ghetto subculture, but are not adaptive for social and economic progress. Again, if blacks survive, blacks can't.

There are several questions raised but left unanswered by Hannerz's study:

1. What do street families do when the "weather does not permit?"
2. What is malfunctional and nonadaptive about a social system that has few barriers to belonging? (Perhaps the problem is that it permits access to social science researchers.)

3. How different are Hannerz's swingers from young people of
   all socio-economic backgrounds in this society? Is that not
   the typical young adult lifestyle he describes?

What I observe in Hannerz's descriptions, which he is unable to
see, is black families at every stage of the life cycle making it
under the conditions with which they are confronted.

There are women with small children who do not have
spacious backyards for their children to play in, but do not
deny their children "fresh air"; whether or not it seems
"respectable," they sit on the stoops or steps watching their
children in the streets. In the typical households he describes,
I see mutual support systems, grandmothers with useful roles,
continuity between the present and the past, women sharing
child-care responsibilities and relieving the burden associated
with multiple roles such as breadwinning, child care, care of
seniors, and community work.

It would be difficult to be a young adult in this society and
not be attracted to the kind of swinger role the author describes.
Such images of successful youth are foisted on young adults by
Hollywood and the media. Many of the swingers described by
Hannerz are young people who go to school and who work to
afford their "clean" cars and "natty" clothing. Such personal
care and grooming flies in the face of stereotypes to which black
people have had to react for centuries, especially "Sambo" with
his lazy careless demeanor and low self-esteem.

A more careful analysis is reported in an ethnographic study of
a lower-class midwestern black community.[23] This analysis of
household and residence patterns among black families whose
style of life is comparable to that of the families whom Hannerz
labeled street families, revealed a kin-based network of exchange
relationships. Individuals in these families usually pool resources,
either through short-term loans to each other or to individuals in
other households. Network members share in child-care tasks,
and individuals are bonded to household units through mutual
obligation. Women in such households usually have children,
and some receive support for them through Aid to Families
with Dependent Children (AFDC). As a group they, therefore,

have more resources for support for themselves and their children than if each of these child-rearing units were to establish individual households. Fathers of their children, although they may maintain their residence in a separate kin-based household, often maintain stable, sexual bonds with the women and also contribute small amounts of money to the support of their children. Because these men may be in precarious employment status, Stack maintains they are often viewed by the women as being "no good" as husbands, but they may be viewed as suitable and desirable boyfriends and fathers. As a case in point, Stack describes the establishment of a nuclear household by one of her respondents, her boyfriend, and their offspring during a period when the man was working. When he was laid off from his job, it soon became essential for the woman and her children to apply for AFDC and to move back into her network of friends and family. The man moved back to his network.

The most stable families in this community are of the extended kin-based type. Thus, Stack argues, these forces militate against the establishment and maintenance of nuclear family units. She reports that many of the black women believe they are obligated to an extended network and must leave only if they meet a so-called good man, and they will be forced to move from the area to, in her words, make a go of it.

While Hannerz has described these same types of households,[24] Stack offers explanations as to how these household structures function to maintain the group.[25] Both researchers use the ethnographic method, and, consequently, the results cannot be generalized but do generate hypotheses about other lower-class groups. Literature that is ethnographic and observational has proven a valuable source of theoretical perspectives that are not influenced by traditional middle-class ethnocentrism. Researchers employing these methods have shown that other institutions in lower-class black communities aid in fulfilling family functions and that fathers, although statistically absent from the household, may have both contact with their children and serve instrumental functions.[26] To what extent these configurations occur in other communities is a question that remains unanswered.

Billingsley, in seeking a theoretical framework within which to encompass the variation in black family life, contends that the black community constitutes an ethnic subsystem of American society.[27] He posits that within this subsystem black families are located variously in social spaces created by the intersection of social class, north-south region, and urban-rural residence. Family structure, he argues, can be classified into twelve types, depending on the presence of children, both spouses, or other kin. These different family structures, he maintains, are responses to oppressive social forces and function to maintain the survival of the group. He argues that these families function to fulfill both instrumental and expressive needs of their members and that variation in the ability of families to secure adequate placement in the larger society results in variation in the family structures which take on the functions necessary to survival.

Although this explanation is sensitive to the various structures that exist among black American families, it precludes creative culture in the black community. Black families brought their traditions of affiliation, mutual support, and extendedness with them to the New World. Their ability to see the ultimate interdependence of all humanity flows from the African philosophical influence on the black world view, and it has been manifest in black culture in Africa, in slavery, and in freedom. Manifestations of interdependence are thus not transient reactions to structural conditions.

Hsu maintains that such differences in Eastern and Western philosophical systems can be observed in cultural patterns and are carried over to the values in research.[28] He shows, for example, that attitudes of Western adults toward their parents are influenced and validated by Judeo-Christian religion. He cites the case of Noah who was instructed to take his wife, sons, and animals aboard the ark, but whose parents were left to drown.

It is true that black families are greatly influenced by Western philosophical systems, but their roots are in Eastern ones. One set of values cannot be measured at the expense of others. How do these sets of values interact? What do black families take from both worlds to act upon their existence?

In an attempt to test Billingsley's theory that the black family takes on structural forms to fulfill three types of functions, Williams interviewed 321 out of a neighborhood of 324 black households.[29] He classified household types according to Billingsley's typology[30] and found that 60 percent of the households could be classified according to his scheme. Williams agrees with Billingsley that traditional definitions of the family would not incorporate these family groups. Using the same measure of family functions, Williams cross-tabulated family structure by instrumental functions. He found that a smaller percentage of husband-wife families without children had high school diplomas and full-time jobs than did husband-wife families with children. This difference is attributed to the presence of aged couples in the sample without children. Williams also found that attenuated-extended families, those which were most often a parent or parents with a daughter and one or more children, have less money per family member, but better housing than families of women and children alone.

As regards expressive functions, such as belonging, self-worth, adjustment to the marital role, companionship of husbands and wives, and cohesion, there are few differences among traditional nuclear families. Husband-wife families living in the household of parents felt the greatest sense of belonging of all. Women and children living with grandparents felt the least satisfied with expressive relationships. Women in these families had lower self-esteem scores than others. The author suggests that this type of family may be less capable of fulfilling the expressive family function and that such families may experience conflict and role strain. All types of families desired college educations for their children and expected that they would obtain them.

Nuclear families with children in school had significantly fewer school problems than other types of families. They were more likely to view children as positive additions to their families and to feel that they were good parents. Women in families with children and grandparents were less likely to have problems with their children than were women with children alone, suggesting that the presence of grandparents represents support systems that help the healthy development of children.

The grandparent extended family with a woman and her children is more likely to report emotional problems with its children, however. Again this finding raises the question of the extent to which conflict may characterize some of these families.

Williams finds support for Billingsley's structural variation, but questions the abilities of the various family forms to function. Broken families, although some may be more functional than others, appear to be considerably less functional than other types.

Williams concludes that by the measures of survival level functioning, which include "per capita income," amount of food money, and adequacy of housing, that none of the types, including the socially valued nuclear family type, seemed to be fulfilling these functions. It is reasonable then to assume that inability to provide survival level resources to the family may underlie conflict and expressive relationships. Williams concludes that the source of the problem lies not in family structure but in the larger society.[31]

This study highlights the complexity of the problems that come into play under conditions of economic depression. For example, the study suggests that the single parent family, in seeking better housing and child care, may be forced to trade them for peace of mind and guilt. The study does not test for interactions that are suggested by the issue, however. That is, when families are together and making money, are they also fulfilling expressive functions? Williams's research represents significant progress in the area of black family studies and shows that many of the major propositions in this area are amenable to quantitative research. It is flawed, however, by many of the methodological problems that characterize research on black Americans. In discussing the problems of families, the study does not define the extent to which these issues are problems. It just reports ordinal relationships. For example, the researcher does not say to what extent the respondents' children have emotional problems. Instead, he simply reports that the parents were *more* likely to report such problems.

Lammermeier, a social historian, used a modified version of Billingsley's typology of family structure to see if the nineteenth-century black family was as matriarchal as reported by Frazier.[32]

He analyzed census data for the period 1850 to 1880 and found that during that period only 21 percent of black families in the Ohio Valley were female headed. After slavery there was an increase in two-parent families, and over 96 percent of the male heads listed occupations. Overwhelmingly, between 1850 and 1880, both nuclear families and extended-augmented families had male heads. Lammermeier's and Billingsley's statistics show an increasing tendency for nuclear households to assume the mother-father-children structure, while, at the same time, the extended-augmented families were becoming increasingly female headed. As this tendency did not become apparent until the 1870s, Lammermeier argues, the causal nexus of black family breakup was apparently not slavery, but instead the poverty and discrimination placed on these families by urban life. These data contradict the earliest interpretations of black family life, which argue that marital instability, matriarchy, and other factors attributed to blacks were family configurations caused by slavery and part of the cultural heritage of black society.

To some extent Lammermeier's contemporary socio-historical research contains a covert statement regarding the ultimate locus of family theory and research in this philosophical and technological era. His application of correlational techniques to historical data yields no support for the theses that were generated in that era and supported by the research of that time. This discrepancy, however, can be attributed to the differences in research methods employed; that is, most of the propositions were born in an era when the method of socio-historical explanation was more intuitive than scientific. The historical paradigms, although intuitively based and invalid, were carried over to research on black Americans.

This work has attempted to reconstruct that socially created and scientifically documented reality of black families as it pertains to areas of black family life in which stereotypes have taken on the status of truths.

From these myths, science has constructed research models, and tested them, often giving so-called scientific validity to conclusions of poorly conducted research. These findings have been operationalized into policy, however, and black families have been defamed and maligned by societal institutions.

1. Absent fathers are pursued at exorbitant costs and often at the expense of another family that will be destroyed when he is located.
2. Black women, who must identify the absent fathers, if they need support, are submitted to degradation and shame.
3. Black men and women in prison cannot be visited by their families if they do not fit legal definitions of families.
4. Black fathers without resources are often imprisoned—which does not help either the mother or the child, who might benefit from a father's affection if not his money.

Overwhelmingly, however, black women and their children are self-supporting. The strengths of black families, whether one-parent, two-parent, or extended, are manifest in their intergenerational ability: (1) to educate more and more of their members, (2) to maintain themselves in spite of structurally sustained unemployment, and discrimination in employment and wages, (3) to move into more significant and active roles in local, national, and international spheres, and (4) to provide support for their members in the face of continuing hostile structural responses to their race and to their needs as humans.

Yet policy does not incorporate these strengths. Despite the fact that three-fourths of black children who are raised by persons other than their parents are raised successfully—whether by aunts, grandparents, uncles, siblings, quasi kin, or women who just "raise children"—public adoption and placement agencies often determine such families to be ineligible for the placement of black children. Black families are, therefore, bypassed in the placement of black children, and black children have been relegated to institutions, to white families, and to Jonestown, Guyana.

NOTES

1. See Robert B. Hill, regarding adoption policies, *Informal Adoption Among Black Families.* Washington, D.C.: National Urban League Research Department. 1977.

2. See U.S. Department of Commerce, Bureau of the Census, *Marital Status and Living Arrangements: March 1979;* and U.S. Department of

Commerce, Bureau of the Census, *American Families and Living Arrangements.* May 1980.

3. Moynihan, *The Negro Family.*

4. Ibid.

5. J. Richard Udry, "Marital Instability by Race, Sex, Education, and Occupation Using 1960 Census Data." *American Journal of Sociology.* 72:203-209. 1967.

6. J. Richard Udry, "Marital Instability by Race and Income Based on 1960 Census Data." *American Journal of Sociology.* 72:673-674. 1967.

7. Jessie Bernard, "Marital Stability and Patterns of Status Variables." *Journal of Marriage and the Family.* 28(11):421-439. 1966.

8. See also Lee Rainwater, *Behind Ghetto Walls: Black Family Life in a Ghetto Slum.* Chicago: Aldine. 1970.

9. R. A. Schermerhorn, "Comment on Bernard." *Journal of Marriage and the Family.* 28:440-442. 1966.

10. Lee Rainwater, "Comment on Bernard." *Journal of Marriage and the Family.* 28:442-445. 1966.

11. Catherine Chilman, "Comment on Bernard." *Journal of Marriage and the Family.* 28:446-448. 1966.

12. Thomas P. Monahan, "Family Fugitives." *Marriage and Family Living.* 20:146-151. 1958.

13. Greto Miao, "Marital Instability and Unemployment Among Whites and Nonwhites, the Moynihan Report Revisited—Again." *Journal of Marriage and the Family.* 36:77-86. 1974.

14. Moynihan, *The Negro Family.*

15. Beverly Duncan and Otis Dudley Duncan, "Family Stability and Occupational Success." *Social Problems.* 16:273-285. 1969.

16. Elizabeth Herzog, "Is There a Breakdown of the Negro Family?" *Social Work.* 11:3-10.

17. Charles V. Willie and Janet Weinandy, "The Structure and Composition of 'Problem' and 'Stable' Families in a Low-Income Population." In Charles V. Willie, ed., *The Family Life of Black People.* Columbus, Ohio: Charles E. Merrill. 1970.

18. Rainwater, *Behind Ghetto Walls.*

19. Jessie Bernard, *Marriage and Family Among Negroes.* Englewood Cliffs, N.J.: Prentice-Hall. 1968.

20. Ibid.

21. Ulf Hannerz, *Soulside: Inquiries into Ghetto Culture and Community.* New York: Columbia University Press. 1969.

22. Ibid.

23. Stack, *All Our Kin.*

24. Hannerz, *Soulside.*

25. Stack, *All Our Kin.*

26. Ford, "Case Studies."

27. Andrew Billingsley, *Black Families in White America.* Englewood Cliffs, N.J.: Prentice-Hall. 1968.

28. Francis L. K. Hsu, "Roots of the American Family: From Noah to Now." In Allan J. Lichtman and Joan R. Challinor, eds., *Kin and Communities.* Washington, D.C.: Smithsonian Institution Press. 1979.

29. Allen J. Williams, Jr., and Robert Stockton, "Black Family Structures and Functions: An Empirical Examination of Some Suggestions Made by Billingsley." *Journal of Marriage and the Family.* 35(1):39-49. 1973.

30. Billingsley, "Black Families."

31. Williams and Stockton, "Black Family Structures and Functions."

32. Paul J. Lammermeier, "The Urban Black Family of the Nineteenth Century: A Study of Black Family Structure in the Ohio Valley, 1850-1880." *Journal of Marriage and the Family.* 35:440-456. 1973; Frazier, *The Negro Family in the United States.*

9

Summary

Hill and Hansen favor collapsing the institutional and structural-functional frameworks of family analysis into one category and the situational and interactional perspectives into another, based on the similarities in their primary concerns.[1] The developmental framework uses the concepts of both of these perspectives and thus can be superimposed on either, depending on the interests of the investigator.

Those studies that have been done of the black family from the institutional or the structural functional perspective, or from both perspectives, have focused primarily on family structures and functions, and interpretations of these studies have been colored by the belief that Western families have evolved the "best" family form for fulfilling the requirements of their society. The greater prevalence of female-headed black families than of female-headed white families stimulated theories that proposed the causes of black pathology rates to lie in family structure, since it is families that transmit culture and, by so doing, "place" their children in the broader social milieu. In focusing on the structure and functions of this group, some researchers of this leaning ignored intragroup variance in Afro-American society and generated propositions regarding the detrimental effects of what they called the "matriarchal character of black society" and the malfunctioning of black families.

The fallacies in their approach lay not in the theory, but in the failure of those who use it to test it empirically. This failure is evidenced in recent studies of Gutman and

Genovese whose analyses of historical data find no support for either the theorized causes of matriarchy or its prevalence in the historical era upon which such propositions were based.[2] Such fallacy is also highlighted by studies that find gross inequalities in the occupational placement of black and white men who are matched on two-parent family of orientation structure and education.[3] Deduced from such studies are the propositions that:

1. The placement requirements of the society are different for blacks and whites.
2. When black socialization and educational requirements are fulfilled, they are for placement at the lower rungs in the occupational ladder.

Billingsley took this position when he treated black America as an ethnic subsystem of American society and argued that the requirements of this subsystem imposed by the larger society have been met through a range of functional adaptations in family structures.[4] An empirical test of Billingsley's propositions, however, did bear out his theory of family structures, although it did not support his theory of, what he called, "functionality."[5] In attempting to bridge these two positions, Rainwater argues that the cultural material prevalent in black ghetto families is functional for survival in that milieu, but malfunctional in the broader society.[6] This position, too, assumes that societal and subsocietal requirements are different, an important point to note and one that is reflective of the "damned-if-you-do, damned-if-you-don't" perspective which social scientists often focus on black families. Anthropologists, who often take the position that adaptive cultural materials persist, view structural adaptations in black families as functional and as being directly related to the socio-economic imperatives of the wider American society.[7] Matrifocality, they argue, is an adaptation to specific and known material conditions. More recent research has buttressed black family functions with African philosophical underpinnings.[8]

These contrary positions differ only in their assumptions of what is functional, and to that extent they are more ideologically than intellectually different. Despite the vast literature already generated by structural, functional, and institutional investigators, we still know little of how structurally differentiated black families function in American society as a whole or of how these structures articulate with their cultures and with the structure and ideology of the American economic system; there has, however, been some indication that relationships among the entities exist.[9] There is more evidence than counterevidence that familial roles are conditioned by economic roles and by the ideology and rationalization which support them.[10] And, to that extent, differences in family roles between black and white families imply economic and cultural interactions and not racial causality.

Findings regarding differences in black and white sexual behavior leave this investigator with one remaining question—so what?[11] Sexual behavior has not been *causally* related to such attributes or behaviors as family structures, roles, or functions, and recently psychopathologists have been relating sexual "restraint" to black and white mental illness. Overwhelmingly, the causes of differences in black and white orientation toward their own sexuality appear to be contemporary ideological differences, although in traditional African culture, sex is treated as a natural human imperative. Researchers interested in explaining contemporary American social life must also acknowledge that once there was an economic imperative for black sexual interaction created by the chattel system of slavery within which such interaction was valued for its contribution to labor.

Studies of black American families that have primarily focused on the interactional patterns in family functioning have done so without respect to external influences. Research concerning role performance remains highly inconclusive. Some of the studies base their conclusions that black families are matriarchal on impressionistic data;[12] some researchers base their conclusions on questionable interpretations of their data;[13] and there are as many studies that find no evidence of matriarchy as there are studies that find such evidence.[14] An overview of this research leads this investigator to conclude that these inconsistencies result in large part from different methodologies, which include differences in assumptions, concepts, hypotheses, methods, and especially in the value positions of the researchers.

Research into marital satisfaction finds evidence that black wives are less satisfied or less enthusiastic about their marriages than are white wives.[15] Such satisfaction, however, is found to be contingent upon a combination of other factors, such as age, presence of children, education, income, labor force participation[16] as well as upon social psychological factors.[17] Since none of these studies reports dissatisfaction with the wives' marriages, the question arises as to whether the lowered enthusiasm of black wives might not be more an index of their realistic approach to marriage than of anything else. While there are higher rates of marital disruption among blacks, no studies as yet have correlated marital satisfaction and disruption for individuals; these factors are simply assumed to be negatively related. We should not preclude the possibility that if the reports of marital satisfaction were analyzed in relation to disrupted marriages, the findings might show that those whose marriages dissolve include wives who are less realistic in evaluating their marriages. If sex roles and marital satisfaction are, in fact, linked to marital disruption, this relationship has not been substantiated empirically. There have been no studies that have interviewed randomly selected mates from broken and stable marriages to seek the causes of disruption and stability. Any propositions regarding these relationships have been based on ecological, not individual, correlations.

While it has been argued that the internal dynamics of black families are such that they represent an undesirable milieu for the socialization of their children, the evidence is slight. Studies of child-rearing families, assuming these to be pathological milieux, have focused on child-rearing practices and the development of adolescent identity consistent with a preconceived notion. Overwhelmingly, the literature on child-rearing practices shows these to be class and culture, not race, related, although such effects often have been obscured by researchers who do not introduce class and culture controls.[18] Child-rearing differences in black and white families have also been related to the differences in exposure these families have to child-rearing literature[19] and to differences in social mobility.[20] Both exposure and mobility, however, are conditioned by social class and culture. Whether different behavioral outcomes are the direct result of these different factors, however, remains undiscerned, since this research has been concentrated on samples who are rearing children of an age at which such effects would not be observable. Researchers carrying their own different values into studies of black child rearing characterize black socialization in different ways: (1) in early childhood as focused in the direction of valuing persons and people rather than material and status, and (2) in later childhood as structurally influenced, taking into account the quest for materials and its interaction with racism.[21]

Although the child-rearing practices of black families have not been empirically linked to the development of adolescent identity, investigators of "identity" have been guided by the assumption that they are, in fact, linked.[22] Stephens[23] and Cavan[24] offer only impressionistic evidence that interactional patterns influenced by the matriarchal structure of black families cause personality disorders, delinquency, and effeminate males, yet these researchers have often been cited in the literature.

Students concentrating on the effects of father absence on adolescent identification interpret their findings as evidence that blacks and father-absent boys, while they may be overtly masculine, have an underlying "feminine identification."[25] The feminine identification measure is based solely on responses to the "IT" scale, which may be a culturally biased instrument in that it asks subjects to state their preference for such matters as toys and roles, which the researchers assume should be preferable to one sex. That is to say, that in the opinion of this investigator, black and white males might conceivably not perceive the identical thing in the role of an Indian chief, and their preference for such a role might be conditioned by their placement in society. A view of underlying feminine identification persists, however, despite the nature of the evidence and, when challenged by evidence of overt masculine behavior, is supported by the theory of "compensatory masculinity," which is a much less verifiable concept.

Research into children's perceptions of adult roles shows that, overwhelmingly, black and white young children and adolescents tend to view males as having the traditional breadwinner role.[26] Black adolescent males and adults, however, have been noted to state their preference for more egalitarian role structures.[27] Except for the research that proffers "compensatory masculinity" theses as explanations of negative findings, the most safe conclusion from this area of research is that black and white one-parent and two-parent males do not differ significantly with respect to sex role perceptions or behavior, except that black men are more likely to incorporate respect and value for the work contributed by their wives and mothers. From the information reported in these studies, it is not even possible to tell whether "IT" scale scores are significantly different for blacks and whites. The investigators simply report their ordinal positions on the scales.[28] An overview of the above research shows that the major conclusions derived from such research do not have an empirical basis and are not always logically consistent; they may, therefore, be questioned on either empirical or logical grounds, or on both.

NOTES

1. Hill and Hansen, "The Identification of Conceptual Frameworks."
2. Gutman, *The Black Family in Slavery and Freedom;* Genovese, *Roll Jordan Roll;* and Lammermeier, "The Urban Black Family."
3. Duncan and Duncan, "Family Stability."
4. Billingsley, "Black Families."
5. Williams and Stockton, "Black Family Structures."
6. Rainwater, *Behind Ghetto Walls.*
7. Hannerz, *Soulside;* Stack, *All Our Kin;* and Charles A. Valentine, *Culture and Poverty.* Chicago: University of Chicago Press. 1968.
8. Nobles, "Africanity."
9. Miao, "Marital Instability"; Duncan and Duncan, "Family Stability"; Liebow, *Tally's Corner;* and Stack, *All Our Kin.*
10. Ibid.
11. See especially Reiss, "Premarital Sexual Permissiveness"; Ladner, *Tomorrow's Tomorrow;* and Schulz, *Coming Up Black.*
12. Moynihan, *The Negro Family;* Brink and Harris, *Black and White;* and Schwartz, "Northern U.S. Negro Matriarchy."
13. Blood and Wolfe, *Husbands and Wives;* and Axelson, "The Working Wife."

14. Scanzoni, "Sex Roles"; Middleton and Putney, "Dominance in Decisions"; and Hyman and Reed, "Black Matriarchy Reconsidered."

15. Blood and Wolfe, *Husbands and Wives*; Rainwater, "Crucible"; and Karen S. Renne, "Correlates of Dissatisfaction in Marriage." *Journal of Marriage and the Family*. 32:54-66. 1970; Lopata, *Occupation Housewife*; and Scanzoni, "Sex Roles."

16. Renne, "Correlates"; and Scanzoni, "Sex Roles."

17. Scanzoni, "Sex Roles."

18. Davis and Havighurst, "Social Class and Color Differences"; Radin and Kamii, "Child Rearing Attitudes"; and Kamii and Radin, "Class Differences."

19. Blau, "Exposure."

20. Zena Smith Blau, "Class Structures, Mobility and Change in Child Rearing." *Sociometry*. 28:210-219. 1965.

21. Lewis, "Black Family: Socialization."

22. Dai, "Some Problems in Personality Development."

23. Stephens, "Judgement by Social Workers."

24. Cavan, "Negro Family Disorganization."

25. Hetherington, "Effects of Paternal Absence."

26. Aldous, "Children's Perceptions"; and Baughman and Dahlstrom, *Negro and White Children*.

27. Frumkin, "Attitudes"; and King, "Adolescent Perceptions."

28. Hetherington, "Effects"; Barclay and Cusumano, "Father Absence"; and Biller, "A Note on Father Absence."

10

Methodological Problems in the Study of Black Families

Two major works in the sociology of sociology have titles which are pertinent to the methodological issues involved in black family research—one, *Knowledge For What?*, the other, *Knowledge From What?*[1]

Knowledge for what? speaks to the questions of why we want the knowledge we seek about a group or population. In what way will the knowledge be useful? *How* might it be used? The insistence that sociology remain pure, that its data and knowledge be garnered for academic purposes is a pathetic answer, especially as positive practical uses of social science might be considered. It is particularly important that the question be answered explicitly when dealing with politically and economically depressed populations, among which black families are salient.

Failure to point out the political nature of observed social conditions and to bring scientific expertise to bear in delineating possible corrective measures suggests itself to be inhumane, since the consequences of nonaction may be as devastating as acts intended to exacerbate conditions. To insist that the desire to correct social problems is the concern of social workers and not of sociologists is to ignore our own ties with society and to, perhaps, place ourselves above the world, looking down. Such a stance may suggest objectivity to the uncritical, but one need only to look around to see that all of mankind is subjectively involved with the rest, and the futures of all groups are intimately interwoven in the fabric of human survival. To suggest that data which indicate that one-third of all black Americans live below the official poverty level are facts of only academic interest is ludicrous, especially when such knowledge contributes to our ability to ameliorate the conditions. Is it through such a stance that social scientists serve the status quo?

Researchers who make claim to seeking "knowledge for knowledge's sake" forget that they often justify the potential use of the taxpayers' dollars in support of their research by alluding to the implications their proposed research findings will have for social reform and social policy. Every reviewer of the potentially funded proposal should be forced by society to ask the questions of that proposed research, "Knowledge *for* what?" It is likely that among the alternatives is an interesting set of answers. Shall we seek knowledge to alleviate oppression and its conditions, or shall we passively remain "academic," reify oppression, and let that state run its course?

Since the research enterprise ideally should begin and end with an examination of theory, the issue "Knowledge *from* what?" should begin at the point of conceptualization. To some extent it is fair to argue that models of social reality that have been applied in the study of black families have been standardized across the experience of a majority of Americans and have been guided by the ideologies that support the status quo. Attempts to compare black families to white families have, therefore, been lodged in theoretical orientations that assume equal opportunity for all Americans to conform to the patterns that are idealized in American culture. Such approaches assume a uniformity of historical, cultural, and contemporary experience and, therefore, attempt to assess the quality of the black experience in the same manner and using the same instruments as in the study of the modal American experience. Using race as an independent variable in this manner does not yield data that can be used to alleviate much of the agony associated with the black condition and does little more than lead to individuous comparisons. I contend, as well, that such comparisons serve to obscure the role of other variables that give meaning to the concept of race, namely, racism and discrimination. Let me clarify this idea.

As students of elementary statistics, most of us have been taught and can, to some extent, take for granted the notion that *nothing* can be assumed to be prior to "race" in a causal model. Simultaneously, it has been argued by methodologists that the concept of race has "face validity." The rationale for these propositions is, of course, the taken-for-granted, mundane understanding that one is born with one's race, and, consequently, race can only be conceived of as an exogenous influence without social antecedents. Race, like sex, is one of the few variables for which we require no conceptual definition. It is my position that this is a fallacy by which we all have been duped, and, in so being, we have failed to measure or consider the antecedents to race.

What is race? Biologically, race is a classificatory category to which we assign persons based on the phenotypic expression of genetically transmitted characteristics relating to skin color, hair, body, and facial characteristics that are shared more with persons in one geographic area than in others. Or, a race is a geographic group of people among whom a higher frequency of genes for physical traits like skin color, hair, facial, and body structure exist than for other geographic groups. Using gene frequency as the criteria for race, siblings of one biologically white and one biologically black parent, depending on the degree of blackness or whiteness in their appearance vis-à-vis these traits, might be considered as members of different races; and depending on the genetic material they pass on to their offspring, it is conceivable that the offspring could be of a different race than the parent. While this may seem absurd, it serves to highlight the fact that there is no scientifically sound way of measuring race as a biological concept. What then is race? Ashley Montagu argues that race is "man's most dangerous myth."[2] What is myth? From Webster, "any imaginary person or thing spoken of as though existing."[3] Conceptualizing race as the myth that it is, rather than as the biological entity it is not, allows for the possibility of its antecedents. What possibly could precede a myth in a causal process? It should not require an astute observer to see that the concept of race is given meaning only through the existence of racism.

Harris and others have pointed out that in Brazil, where there are many different racial mixtures, people are more likely to be stratified on the basis of socio-economic class than on any other basis and that there is much ambiguity in the assignment of persons of varying phenotypes to racial categories.[4] That is to say, there is no reason that we should believe race causes racism, and not vice versa. In fact, in relatively homogenous societies, the concept of race has no meaning and the comparison of nonwhites to whites is not salient in the research enterprise. We are, therefore, suggesting that the measurement of race without its antecedents is meaningless, and variance in dependent variables that we assume to result from race may, in actuality, be the spurious consequence of racism. In any case, what does it tell us to know that there is a statistical deviation between black families and white families on any characteristic. Isn't statistical normality an artifact of the size of the population that makes up a distribution? It is like arguing that black families, because they are not white families, are different. It is because such statistical deviance has been treated as de facto deviance that I have felt it necessary to elaborate to this extent on the fallacy of such models of reality.

SAMPLING

In addition to some of the logical weaknesses referred to above, the validity of data on black American families has been affected by techniques that are utilized to select samples from which researchers may generalize findings to the majority U.S. population. The cost of such generalizations to the minority group, because of segregation of the poor and their residential clustering in our society, is significant. Another factor affecting the representation of black samples is the dispersion of black middle to upper classes within residential districts chiefly inhabited by "majority" populations. Consequently, black families, within the context of national, and other, probability samples, have been over-whelmingly characterized as, among other things, lower class, living in public or substandard housing, and part of broken families. This depiction has led to an American cultural distortion, inasmuch as the majority of the American population takes for granted that the characteristics of these biased samples can, in fact, be generalized to the entire black population.

At present, there exists no sampling frame that may be employed to ensure that every member of the black population has an equal probability of being selected. This is a fact of minority status. There are no exhaustive lists of the black population from which we can get a simple random sample. Neither are there criteria along which we may stratify to ensure a probability sample of blacks whose distribution of socio-economic characteristics is equal to black population proportions. While some studies have overselected blacks in predominantly white areas in order to obtain what the researchers see as more relevant data, there has as yet been no analysis that assesses their relevance. It is our position that sampling constraints imposed in previous studies which have included blacks as sub-samples have also influenced the observed deficit in quality data on black families and have, instead, generated data of questionable utility.

MEASUREMENT

Among the measurement deficiencies observed in the study of black families are those in instruments designed to study and compare the psychological status of black and white youth. While it may be possible to find a list of universal events, ideas, sentiments, and other conditions that affect the psychological orientations of both minorities and nonminorities, that list would not be exhaustive for the population. Weems and Sizemore suggest that many factors that foster the well-being and, therefore, the psychological orientation of whites may depress the well-being of blacks.[5] As an empirical example, Counter has found that the Afro-Americans of Surinam, because of their historical experience, define their well-being and life satisfaction as being directly related to the distance they maintain from the white population.[6] It, therefore, would be absurd to measure their life satisfaction on the same scale as that of the white Surinamese. While this example may be extreme, it highlights the relationship between mental states, which we treat as being relatively static, and past experience.

Nobles, in his work on the philosophical underpinnings of black institutional life, points out how peculiarly the Afro-American experience with American racism and discrimination has shaped black definitions of reality.[7] His work suggests that the events, ideas, and other matters given importance by many Afro-Americans are often different from those of many other Americans. These experiential antecedents are important determinants of response to our models. Ordinal scales, in that they have no "zero point," may obscure differences in the way blacks and whites respond to the same material. That is, it is impossible to determine whether two groups with so widely variant experience as blacks and whites are responding to a scale item in the same way when given choices of, for example, "very happy," "happy," "pretty happy," "unhappy," or "very unhappy." It is unclear as to whether the choice, "very happy," for one group, or person for that matter, is different from the choice "pretty happy" for another. My contention is that the use of ordinal scale data to compare groups of so different experience only exacerbates problems of interpretation.

DATA MANIPULATION

Again, I address the problem of the assumption of equal opportunity, this time with respect to data manipulation. Guided by such assumptions, many researchers have sought to explain variance in outcome variables as being the function of the character, either genetic or cultural, of the black population. The methods of research applied to the test of such hypotheses have covered a broad spectrum. These methods have included: (1) uncontrolled observations of variance, as in naturalistic settings, with the findings generalized to the entire population of black families; (2) tabular analyses of data derived from large or small samples, using race as an independent variable, but limited by the inability to interpret relationships of a very high order; and (3) linear analyses of data, as in multiple regression and path analysis which, while they permit statistical control of many more variables, become problematic in use with minorities. Some issues using these methods are explicated below.

Consistent with my concern with the effect of "N" size on measures of central tendency (which, incidentally, is analagous to the problem of being a minority, that is, inability to define the norm), I feel compelled to criticize the use—or misuse—of the linear model in comparisons of black to white samples. Rarely do data meet the assumptions underlying the linear model, and, while the cost to *all* of the data may be minimal, the costs to minority data are devastating. This is a direct effect of the "N size-normality" relationship. Use of regression analysis, for example, assumes certain characteristics of the data, which, while they may be met for white samples, are rarely met for blacks. The analysis of the mean and deviations around it, assume that the dependent variable is normally distributed at each value of the independent variable. While such dependent variables as occupation and income may be normally distributed for whites, they are negatively skewed for blacks, thus affecting the validity of the use of this model (see figure 10.1).

The assumption of linearity associated with this model is also highly suspect when it comes to the study of black Americans. It is almost intuitive that the effects of being both poor and black on a single individual may be greater than the effect of being poor on one individual added to the effect of being black on another. While it is possible to add such interaction terms to regression models, researchers rarely bother. It is not surprising then that the findings of major studies employing linear models in black-white comparisons have been subject to controversy and criticism.[8]

FIGURE 10.1

Distribution of Black and White Median Family Income, March, 1979

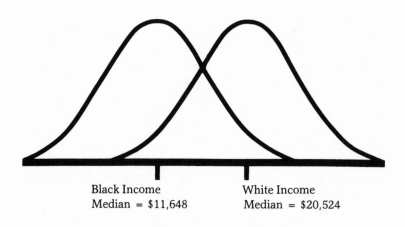

Black Income
Median = $11,648

White Income
Median = $20,524

There is some basis on which we may argue that poverty is America's great social leveller. American families of all races and ethnic backgrounds have a greater probability of being mistreated by social science if they are poor.[9] Again, I contend, however, that such comparisons should be met with skepticism. When the comparisons of black and nonblack families are the explicit aim of the researcher, we should all ask, "Knowledge *for* what?" Will such models be useful for constructing models of successful families? If not, then the motives become even more suspect, and the question "Knowledge *from* what?" demands an honest and critical answer.

I further contend that serious researchers will generate valid and sensitive data on black American families only if they address these methodological issues scrupulously and work to develop sampling frames and quality instruments.

NOTES

1. Robert S. Lynd, *Knowledge For What?* New York: Grove Press. 1964; and Derek L. Phillips, *Knowledge From What?* Chicago: Rand McNally. 1971.

2. Ashley Montagu, *Man's Most Dangerous Myth: The Fallacy of Race.* 5th edition. New York: Oxford University Press. 1974.

3. *Webster's New World Dictionary of the American Language.* Second college edition, s.v. "myth."

4. Marvin Harris, *Culture, People, Nature.* New York: Crowell, 1975.

5. Luther Weems, "Black Community Research Needs: Methods, Models, and Modalities." In Lawrence Gary, ed., *Social Research and the Black Community: Selected Issues and Priorities.* Washington, D.C.: Institute for Urban Affairs and Research. 1974. Pages 25-38. See also Barbara A. Sizemore, "Social Science and Education for a Black Identity." In James A. Banks and Jean D. Grambs, eds., *Black Self-Concept.* New York: McGraw-Hill. 1972.

6. Alan Counter, Symposium.

7. Wade W. Nobles, "African Root and American Fruit: The Black Family." *Journal of Social and Behavioral Sciences.* 20:52-64; and *Formulative and Empirical Study.*

8. See, for example, Christopher Jencks, et al., *Inequality.* New York: Harper Colophon. 1972. Howard F. Taylor, "Playing the Dozens with

Path Analysis: Methodological Pitfalls in Jencks, et al., *Inequality."*
Sociology of Education. Fall: 433-450. 1973; and James S. Coleman, et al.,
Equality of Educational Opportunity. Washington, D.C.: U.S. Department
of Health, Education and Welfare, Office of Education. 1966.

9. For example, the following description is of lower-class *white* families:

> The husband wife relationship is more or less an unstable one. . . . exploitative
> sex liaisons between males from the higher classes frequently occur with
> teenage girls, but they rarely result in marriage. . . . one-fifth to one-fourth
> of all births are illegitimate.

See August Hollingshead, *Elmstown's Youth.* New York: John Wiley.
1949. Page 116.

11

Conclusions

The tenability of the black family as a system that fosters the healthy development of its members has always been at risk. Yet, the functions of the black family have been historically those held by families universally. Added to those functions are others that are the consequence of the interaction of black culture with historical and contemporary racism.

While there are limited opportunities for black families to obtain food, clothing, and shelter for their members, there is little evident recognition of blacks as human beings who have the same needs as others for emotional and sexual gratification. Neither is there apparent awareness that black families have had to incorporate a racist reality into their family ethos and to protect their members from responses to their race. The healthy development of any individual, organization, or family depends upon its responses to its internal and external demands and pressures. Effective growth flows from the ability to incorporate feedback, to change structural patterns and relationships to meet demands, and to establish goals in the direction of greater development.

To some extent, black families have been caught up in the dialectic posed by a racist society. In our own defense we black families have been seduced into postures that do not permit our self-analysis. Our research has been reactive, rather than definitive.

Feedback to black families, therefore, has been conflicting and of little use in their development. Black families have needed to know how to prepare their members for survival and success in a system that has an ethos that ignores black humanity.[1] As a consequence, socialization for success in the American system has meant teaching black family members to value education, occupational achievement, functional relationships, money, and material manifestations of success. Socialization for survival has meant teaching black family members to value people, interdependence, affectional relationships, and religion. Both sets of values have been expressed alone and simultaneously by black families, and both sets of values are functional in the milieux that reward them. Less affluent black families have, therefore, been observed to be more extended, to adopt members informally, and to celebrate family reunions.[2] Families with greater affluence are more nuclear and focus more on individual than on family success. Bianchi and Farley note that the recent trend is for affluent families among all races to become more nuclear and for the poor to become more extended.[3] Stack and McAdoo have both noted a relationship between kin network and mobility patterns that flows from the interaction of these values.[4] Stack observed the influence of economic capacity on household and kin network formation and observes that, "When economic resources are greatly limited, people need help from as many others as possible. This requires expanding their kin networks—increasing the number of people they hope to be able to count on."[5]

McAdoo, in contrast, notes a depressing effect on mobility of having poor relatives and suggests that the cost of upward mobility may be isolation from poorer relatives.[6] She adds that this may cause antagonism between lower- and middle-class blacks and be a source of mental distress. I would add that the cost of mobility might also be isolation from the values that are more functional for survival than success. The individual thus would be poorly equipped to handle the racism that is endemic in America's "higher" strata.

The fact to be synthesized from both findings is that human life and material life are intimately interrelated, and one does not move in a linear fashion without consequence to the other.

Feedback to black families from American institutional life has been fraught with racism. The media have promoted the stereotypes of black America that flow from the value placed on the materialism of the dominant society. Therefore black families have been portrayed as: (1) mimetically pursuing the trappings of material wealth, however crudely, since this is not part of their heritage; and (2) poor, mother-headed, problem ridden, and ghettoized, but religious, happy, and perhaps extended.

Blacks are also likely to be portrayed as poor, but as in hot pursuit of material wealth by way of drugs and other criminal activity. The black family portraits which have least made their way into our consciousness are of those who, although poor, are stable and striving and those who, although middle and upper class, devote their energies and efforts to improving their communities and sharing their tangible and intangible resources.

Black families and all families must be made aware of the confluence of these values and of how they can be the source of stress and distress. They must synthesize as they may have been taught their mastery of success, but not at the cost of their own survival. Crime, drugs, and other self-destructive agents may be the source of material success, but they do not lead to human success. We cannot have one without the other. Neither should the black mobile families "burn the bridges which carry them across." The person who devalues affectional ties and human wealth will find his/herself emotionally bankrupt and without strength to face material denial and discrimination. High rates of mental illness and suicide have been observed among black youth who have no continuity with the black past and who, thinking racism died back then, find it rearing its ugly contemporary head.

Scientific feedback to black families is rife with the same racism that they are trying to negotiate. As in the past, therefore, the future of black families will depend on blacks' ability to assess themselves and their worlds through the lenses of their own existential realities—and not the realities constructed by social science.

When one considers that the initial stance of black family theory was colored by Darwinian notions of evolutionary progress and took the position that black families are evolving under "civilizing" influences toward better states, one wonders if such evolution has not taken place. That is, the conceptual frameworks generated by "value-free" observations and operationalized in complex multivariate analyses, yield a picture of such an evolutionary progress, but whether that progress should be attributed to "black families" or to the research methodology employed in the study of them is moot. I maintain that theory cannot be better than the empirical world that grounds it, and, as such, conclusions made invalid by faulty methods contribute only to the construction of "primitive" theory. Support for the series of propositions that comprise the theoretical framework applied in research on black families is scant. It is in fact so scant that one wonders if social science does not have a "folklore" of its own that also happens to coincide with the folklore in society. While the task of social scientists seems to be to remove the study of black families from beneath the lens of racism and common sense, and to reduce the seeming accident observed in our condition to some sense of order, it appears that, instead, myth is changed to reality. And rather than explaining the widening hiatus between ideal and real family life, social scientists mythologize that gap into a narrow one. In doing this, they create a normative reality from which black deviance is defined and controlled. What then is social theory? Does it describe ideal or real social life? The two do not always coincide. How do our thoughts as scientists about action relate to our personal fears and needs? If theory is constructed from empirical data, then theory itself must be at least as changing, as dynamic as the behavior it describes. Kaplan reminds us that the unyielding insistence that every new theory must fit those theories already established is characteristic of closed systems of thought and not of science.[7]

In constructing reality to fit theory much of human life and family life has been overlooked in the scientific enterprise. As yet we have only limited answers to questions that seemingly should have been answered long ago. If, for example, human survival requires fertility, which in turn requires sexual interaction, where in the locus of social life should we place sex? Is it a wonder then that there is evidence of ancient ritual being often centered around sex and fertility? And where are our modern rituals of sex and fertility? Rather than backing into sex, marriage, and procreation, shouldn't we openly prepare generations for their role in human survival? While the questions posed are philosophical ones, they remain at the core of life and plead for answers. How they are answered for all human life will in turn shed light on the evolutionary continua of black families in the United States and the world. As has been illustrated in this critical review, the taken-for-granted socially constructed and scientifically documented reality regarding black American families remains highly suspect. While it is somewhat disappointing to find that fifty years of research has yielded so little that is definitive, one gains optimism that the future will be more productive as the philosophical gaps between humankind are bridged in the quest for species survival and as advanced technology facilitates the use of complex designs for the study of complex phenomena.

NOTES

1. See Lewis, "Black Family: Socialization."
2. Billingsley, "Black Families"; and Robert B. Hill, *The Strengths of Black Families.* New York: Emerson Hall. 1972.
3. Bianchi and Farley, "Racial Differences."
4. Stack, *All Our Kin;* and McAdoo, "Factors Related to Stability."
5. Stack, *All Our Kin.*
6. McAdoo, "Factors Related to Stability."
7. Abraham Kaplan, *The Conduct of Inquiry.* Scranton, Pa.: Chandler Publishing Co. 1964.

Bibliography

Abzug, Robert H.
1971 "The Black Family During Reconstruction." in Martin Kilson, Daniel M. Fox, and Nathan I. Huggins, eds., *Key Issues in the Afro-American Experience.* Volume 2. New York: Harcourt Brace Jovanovich.

Adams, A. V., and G. Nestel.
1976 "Interregional Migration, Education and Poverty in the Urban Ghetto: Another Look at Black-White Earnings Differentials." *Review of Economics and Statistics.* 58(May):156-166.

Adams, Bert N., and James E. Butler.
1967 "Occupational Status and Husband-Wife Social Participation." *Social Forces.* 45(6):501-507.

Adams, Paul L., and Jeffrey H. Horovitz.
1980a "Coping Patterns of Mothers of Poor Boys." *Child Psychiatry and Human Development.* 10(3):144-155.
1980b "Psychopathology and Fatherlessness in Poor Boys." *Child Psychiatry and Human Development.* 10(3):135-143.

Agrest, Barbara Finlay.
1978 "First Decades of Freedom—Black Families in a Southern County, 1870 and 1885." *Journal of Marriage and the Family.* 40(4):697-706.

Aldous, Joan.
1969a "Occupational Characteristics and Males' Role Performance in the Family." *Journal of Marriage and the Family.* 31(11): 707-712.
1969b "Wives' Employment Status and Lower-Class Men as Husband-Fathers: Support for the Moynihan Thesis." *Journal of Marriage and the Family.* 31(8):469-476.

1972   "Children's Perceptions of Adult Role Assignment: Father-Absence, Class, Race and Sex Influence." *Journal of Marriage and the Family,* 34:55-65.

Aldridge, Delores P.
1972   "Teaching About Black American Families." *Social Education.* 41(6):484-487.

Allen, Walter R.
1970   "The Search for Applicable Theories of Black Family Life." *Journal of Marriage and the Family.* 32:117-129.
1977   "Economics and Family Organization in the Black Community: Socioeconomic Correlates of Urban Black Family Structure and Composition." *Population Index.* 43(3):422.
1978   "Race, Family Setting and Adolescent Achievement Orientation." *Journal of Negro Education.* 47:230-243.

Anderson, Charles S., and Joseph Himes.
1959   "Dating Values and Norms on a Negro College Campus." *Marriage and Family Living.* (April):227-229.

Anderson, Claud, and Rue L. Comwell.
1977   " 'Black is Beautiful' and the Color Preferences of Afro-American Youth." *Journal of Negro Education.* 46(1):76-88.

Andrew, Gwenn.
1968   "Determinants of Negro Family Decisions in Management of Retardation." *Journal of Marriage and the Family.* 30(11):612-617.

Andrews, Roberta G.
1968   "Permanent Placement of Negro Children Through Quasi-Adoption." *Child Welfare.* 47(12):583-586, 613.

Aschenbrenner, Joyce.
1975   *Lifelines: Black Families in Chicago.* New York: Holt, Rinehart and Winston.

Aseltine, Gwendolyn.
1978   "Family Socialization Perceptions Among Black and White High School Students." *Journal of Negro Education.* 47:256-265.

Ashmore, Richard, ed.
1976   "Black and White in the 1970's." *Journal of Social Issues.* 32:(2).

Aug, Robert G., and Thomas Bright.
1970   "Study of Wed and Unwed Motherhood in Adolescents and Young Adults." *Journal of the American Academy of Child Psychiatry.* 9(10):577-594.

Ausubel, David, and Pearl Ausubel.
1963   "Ego Development Among Segregated Negro Children." In A. Harry Passow, ed., *Education in Depressed Areas.* New York: Teachers College Press.

Axelson, Leland J.
1970   "The Working Wife: Differences in Perceptions Among Negro and White Males." *Journal of Marriage and the Family.* 32(8): 457-465.

Babchuk, Nicholas, and John A. Ballweg.
1972   "Black Family Structure and Primary Relations." *Phylon.* 33(12):334-347.

Babchuk, Nicholas, and Ralph V. Thompson.
1962   "The Voluntary Association of Negroes." *American Sociological Review.* 27(10):647-655.

Baber, Ray E.
1937   "A Study of 325 Mixed Marriages." *American Sociological Review.* 2(10):705-716.

Badaines, Joel.
1976   "Identification, Imitation, and Sex-role Preference in Father-present and Father-absent Black and Chicano Boys." *Journal of Psychology* 92:15-24.

Balkwell, Carolyn, Jack Balswick, and James W. Balkwell.
1979   "Black and White Family Patterns in America." *Journal of Marriage and the Family.* 40(4):743-747.

Ball, John C.
1962   *Social Deviancy and Adolescent Personality: An Analytical Study with the MMPI.* Lexington, Ky.: University of Kentucky Press.

Ballweg, John A.
1969   "Husband-Wife Response Similarities on Evaluative and Non-Evaluative Survey Questions." *Public Opinion Quarterly.* 33: 249-254.

Banks, James A., and Jean D. Grambs, eds.
1972   *Black Self Concept.* New York: McGraw-Hill.

Barclay, A. G., and D. Cusumano.
1967   "Father-Absence, Cross-Sex Identity and Field Dependent Behavior in Male Adolescents." *Child Development.* 38(3):243-250.

Bargarozzi, D. A.
1980   "Family Therapy and the Black Middle-Class: A Neglected Area of Study." *Journal of Marriage and Family Therapy.* 6(2):159-166.

Barnett, Larry D.
1963   "Interracial Marriage in California." *Marriage and Family Living.* 25(11):424-427.

Barnett, Marguerite R., and James A. Hefner, eds.
1976   *Public Policy for the Black Community.* Port Washington, N.Y.: Alfred Publishing Co.

Barrett, Barbara Nelson.
1976   "Enterprising Principles of Counseling the Low-Income Black Family." *Journal of Non-White Concerns.* 5(1):14-22.
Barron, Milton L.
1951   "Research on Intermarriage: A Survey of Accomplishments and Prospects." *American Journal of Sociology.* 57(11):249-255.
1972   ed., *The Blending American: Patterns of Intermarriage.* Chicago: Quadrangle Books.
Batchelder, Alan B.
1964   "Decline in the Relative Income of Negro Men." *Quarterly Journal of Economics.* 78(11):525-548.
1965   "Poverty: The Special Case of the Negro." In Louis A. Ferman, Joyce L. Kornbluh, and Alan Haber, eds., *Poverty in America.* Ann Arbor: University of Michigan Press.
1966   *The Economics of Poverty.* New York: John Wiley and Sons.
Bates, James E., Harry H. Lieberman, and Rodney N. Powell.
1970   "Provisions for Health Care in the Ghetto: The Family Health Team." *American Journal of Public Health.* 60(7): 1222-1225.
Baughman, E. Earl.
1971   *Black Americans.* New York: Academic Press.
Baughman, E. Earl, and W. G. Dahlstrom.
1968   *Negro and White Children: A Psychological Study in the Rural South.* New York: Academic Press.
Bauman, Karl E., and J. Richard Udry.
1972   "Powerlessness and Regularity of Contraception in an Urban Negro Male Sample: A Research Note." *Journal of Marriage and the Family.* 34:112-114.
Bayer, Alan E., and F. Ivan Nye.
1964   "Family Life Education in Florida Public High Schools." *Journal of Marriage and the Family.* 5:182-187.
Beal, Frances M.
1969   "Double Jeopardy: To Be Black and Female." *New Generation.* 5:23-28.
Beasley, Joseph D., et al.
1936   "Attitudes and Knowledge Relevant to Family Planning Among New Orleans Negro Females." *American Journal of Public Health.* 57(11):1847-1857.
Beck, Bernard.
1966   "Welfare as a Moral Category." *Social Problems.* 14:258-277.
Becker, Howard, and Reuben Hill.
1955   *Family, Marriage and Parenthood.* Boston: D. C. Heath.

Beckett, Joyce O.
1976   "Working Wives: A Racial Comparison." *Social Work.* 21(6): 463-471.

Bell, Alan P.
1978   "Black Sexuality: Fact and Fancy." In Robert Staples, ed., *The Black Family: Essays and Studies.* Second edition. Belmont, Calif.: Wadsworth.

Bell, Carolyn Shaw.
1970   *The Economics of the Ghetto.* New York: Pegasus.

Bell, Robert.
1965a   "Lower-Class Negro Mothers and Their Children." *Integrated Education.* 2:23-27.

1965b   "The Negro Lower-Class Mother's Aspirations for Her Children." *Social Forces.* 43(5):493-500.

1969   "The Lower-Class Negro Family in the United States and Britain: Some Comparisons." *Race.* 11(10):173-181.

Bennett, Claude F.
1970   "Lateness of Contraception Among Recipients of Subsidized Family Planning Service." *American Journal of Public Health.* 60(11):2110-2117.

Bennett, William S., and Noel P. Gist.
1964   "Class and Family Influences on Student Aspirations." *Social Forces.* 43:167-173.

Benson, Leonard.
1968   *Fatherhood a Sociological Perspective.* New York: Random House.

Berlin, I.
1978   "Historians and Black Families." *Nation.* 226(10):311-313.

Bernard, Jessie.
1966a   "Marital Stability and Patterns of Status Variables." *Journal of Marriage and the Family.* 28(11):421-439.

1966b   *Marriage and Family Among Negroes.* Englewood Cliffs, N.J.: Prentice-Hall.

1966c   "Note on Educational Homogamy in Negro-White and White-Negro Marriages." *Journal of Marriage and the Family.* 28(8): 274-276.

1975   "Note on Changing Life Styles 1970-1974." *Journal of Marriage and the Family.* 37(8):582-593.

Bianchi, Suzanne M., and Farley Reynolds.
1979   "Racial Differences in Living Arrangements and Solid-Economic Well-Being: An Analysis of Recent Trends." *Journal of Marriage and the Family.* 41(3):537-551.

Biller, H., and L. Borstelmann.
1967   "Masculine Development: An Integrative View." *Merrill-Palmer Quarterly.* 13(10):253-294.

Biller, Henry B.
1968   "A Note on Father Absence and Masculine Development in Lower Class Negro and White Boys." *Child Development.* 39(11): 1003-1006.
1969   "Father Absence and Masculine Development in Lower-Class Negro and White Boys." *Child Development.* 40:539-546.

Biller, Henry, and J. Weiss.
1970   "The Father-Daughter Relationship and the Personality Development of the Female." *Journal of Genetic Psychology.* 116:78-93.

Billingsley, Andrew.
1966   "Illegitimacy Problems of Negro Family Life." In Robert W. Roberts, ed., *The Unwed Mother.* New York: Harper and Row.
1969a   *Black Families in White America.* Englewood Cliffs, N.J.: Prentice-Hall.
1969b   "Family Functioning in the Low-Income Black Community." *Social Casework.* 50(12):563-572.
1970   "Black Families and White Social Science." *Journal of Social Issues.* 26:127-142.
1973   "None Shall Part Us From Each Other: Reflection on Black Family Life During Slavery and Beyond." *Proceedings of the Fifth Annual Conference of the National Association of Black Social Workers.* April 18-21. Pages 78-88.
1974   *Black Families and the Struggle for Survival.* New York: Friendship Press.

Billingsley, Andrew, and Amy Tate Billingsley.
1965   "Negro Family Life in America." *Social Service Review.* 39(9): 310-319.

Billingsley, Andrew, and Marilyn C. Greene.
1974   "Family Life Among the Free Black Population in the 18th Century." *Journal of Social and Behavioral Sciences.* 20:1-18.

Blackwell, James E.
1975   *The Black Community: Diversity and Unity.* New York: Harper and Row.

Blassingame, John.
1972   *The Slave Community.* New York: Oxford University Press.
1973   *Black New Orleans 1860-1880.* Chicago: University of Chicago Press.

Blau, Zena Smith.
1964   "Exposure to Child-Rearing Experts: A Structural Interpretation
         of Class-Color Differences." *American Journal of Sociology.*
         69:596-608.
1965   "Class Structure, Mobility and Change in Child Rearing."
         Sociometry. 28:210-219.
Blood, Robert O.
1963   "The Husband-Wife Relationship." In F. Ivan Nye and Lois
         W. Hoffman, eds., *The Employed Mother in America.* Chicago:
         Rand McNally.
Blood, Robert O, and Donald M. Wolfe.
1960   *Husbands and Wives.* New York: Free Press.
1969   "Negro-White Differences in Blue Collar Marriages in a Northern
         Metropolis." *Social Forces.* 48(9):59-64.
Blumberg, Leonard, and Robert R. Bell.
1959   "Urban Migration and Kinship Ties." *Social Problems.* 6(9):
         328-333.
Bogard, Howard M.
1970   "Follow-up Study of Suicidal Patients Seen in Emergency Room
         Consultation." *American Journal of Psychiatry.* 126(7):1017-1019.
Boggs, James.
1972   "Blacks in the Cities: Agenda for the 70's." *Black Scholar.* 4:50-61.
Bogue, Donald J.
1970   "Family Planning in the Negro Ghettos of Chicago." *The Milbank
         Memorial Fund Quarterly.* 48(4):283-307.
Bonner, Florence.
1974   "Black Women and White Women: A Comparative Analysis of
         Perceptions of Sex Roles for Self, Ideal-Self and the Ideal
         Mate." *The Journal of Afro-American Issues.* 2:237-246.
Bott, Elizabeth.
1957   *Family and Social Network.* London: Tavistock.
Bould, S.
1977   "Black and White Families—Factors Affecting Wives' Contri-
         butions to Family Income Where Husbands' Income Is Low to
         Moderate." *Sociological Quarterly.* 18(4):536-547.
Bowie, C. C.
1948   "The Meaning of the Marriage Contract to 674 Negro Male
         Veterans." *International Journal of Sexology.* 2:42-53.
Bracey, John H., August Meier, and Elliot Rudwick.
1971   *Black Matriarchy: Myth and Reality?* Belmont, Calif.: Wadsworth.

Bracken, Michael B., and Stanislav V. Kasl.
1977   "Differences and Delay in the Decision to Seek Induced Abortion Among Black and White Women." *Social Psychiatry.* 12(2):57-70.

Bradley, S., R. C. Beatty, and E. H. Long, eds.
1967   *The American Tradition in Literature.* Third edition. New York: Grosset and Dunlap.

Braxton, Earl T.
1976   "Structuring the Black Family for Survival and Growth." *Perspectives in Psychiatric Care.* 14(4):165-173.

Braxton, Edward R., and Robert J. Yonker.
1973   "Does Being Urban, Poor, Black, or Female Affect Youth's Knowledge and/or Attitudes Relating to Drugs?" *Journal of School Health.* 43(4):185-189.

Brigham, John C., and Linda W. Giesbrecht.
1976   " 'All in the Family': Racial Attitudes." *Journal of Communications.* 26(4):69-74.

Brimmer, Andrew.
1966   "The Negro in the National Economy." In John P. Davis, ed., *The American Negro Reference Book.* Englewood Cliffs, N.J.: Prentice-Hall.

Brink, William, and Louis Harris.
1967   "The Negro Family." In William Brink and Louis Harris, eds., *Black and White.* New York: Simon and Schuster.

Brodber, Erna, and Nathaniel Wagner.
1970   "The Black Family, Poverty and Family Planning: Anthropological Impressions." *The Family Coordinator.* 19(2):168-172.

Broderick, Carlfred B.
1965   "Social Heterosexual Development Among Urban Negroes and Whites." *Journal of Marriage and the Family.* 27:200-203.
1966   "Sexual Behavior Among Pre-Adolescents." *Journal of Social Issues.* 22:6-22.

Brody, Eugene B.
1963   "Color and Identity Conflict in Young Boys: Observations of Negro Mothers in Urban Baltimore." *Psychiatry.* 26:188-201.

Bromley, David G., and Charles F. Longino, Jr., eds.
1972   *White Racism and Black Americans.* Cambridge, Mass.: Schenkman Publishing Company.

Bronfenbrenner, Urie.
1961   "Some Family Antecedents of Responsibility and Leadership in Adolescents." In R. Petriello and B. M. Bass, eds., *Leadership*

and Interpersonal Behavior. New York: Holt, Rinehart and Winston.

Brook, Judith S., Martin Whiteman, Estelle Peisach, and Martin Deutsch.
1974   "Aspiration Levels of and for Children: Age, Sex, Race and Socioeconomic Correlates." *Journal of Genetic Psychology.* 124: 3-16.

Brooks, Gwendolyn.
1951   "Why Negro Women Leave Home." *Negro Digest.* 9:26-28.

Brooks, Lillies.
1951   "I Didn't Raise My Boy to Be a Fighter." *Negro Digest.* 9:3-6.

Broom, Leonard, and Norval D. Glenn.
1945   'The Family." *Transformation of the Negro American.* New York: Harper and Row. Pages 148-179.

Brown, Daniel G.
1957   "Masculinity-Femininity Development in Children." *Journal of Consulting Psychology.* 21:197-202.

Brown, Josephine V., Roger Bakeman, Patricia A. Snyder, W. Timm Frederickson, Sharon T. Morgan, and Ruth Hepler.
1975   "Interactions of Black Inner-City Mothers with Their Newborn Infants." *Child Development.* 46(3):677-686.

Brown, Robert S.
1974   "Wealth Distribution and Its Impact on Minorities." *Review of Black Political Economy.* 4:27-37.

Brown, W. K.
1977   "Black Female Gangs in Philadelphia." *International Journal of Offenders Therapy.* 21(3):221-228.
1978   "Black Gangs as Family Extensions." *International Journal of Offenders Therapy.* 22(1):39-45.

Burbach, Harold J., and Brent Bridgeman.
1976   "Dimensions of Self-Concept Among Black and White Fifth Grade Children." *Journal of Negro Education.* 45(4):448-458.

Burgess, Ernest W., Harvey J. Locke, and Mary Margaret Thomas.
1971   *The Family from Institution to Companionship.* New York: Van Nostrand Reinhold Company.

Burgess, Jane K.
1970   "The Single-Parent Family: A Social and Sociological Problem." *The Family Coordinator.* 19:137-144.

Burton, R. V., and J. W. M. Whiting.
1961   "The Absent Father and Cross-Sex Identity." *Merrill-Palmer Quarterly.* 7:85-95.

Bush, James A.
1976   "Suicide and Blacks: A Conceptual Framework." *Suicide and Life-Threatening Behavior.* 6(4):216-222.

Butler, Cynthia, and Joseph Doster.
1976   "Sex-Role Learning in the Black Male: Research and Clinical Implications." *Journal of Afro-American Issues.* 4:121-138.

Butler, Reginald O.
1976   "Black Children's Racial Preference, A Selected Review of the Literature." *Journal of Afro-American Issues.* 4:168-171.

Butterman, Catherine M.
1968   "The Multimarriage Family." *Social Casework.* 49:218-221.

Cagle, Lawrence, and Irwin Deutscher.
1970   "Housing Aspirations and Housing Achievement: The Relocation of Poor Families." *Social Problems.* 18:243-256.

Caldwell, Betty M., and Leonard Hersher.
1963   "Mother-Infant Interaction During the First Year of Life." *Merrill-Palmer Quarterly.* 10:114-128.

Caldwell, Betty M., Leonard Hersher, Earle L. Lipton, et al.
1963   "Mother-Infant Interaction in Monomatric and Polymatric Families." *American Journal of Orthopsychiatry.* 33:653-664.

Calhoun, Arthur W.
1919   "The Negro Family Since Emancipation." *A Social History of the American Family,* Vol. III. Cleveland: The Arthur H. Clark Co. Pages 39-64.

Calmek, Maynard.
1970   "Racial Factors in the Counter Transference: The Black Therapist and the Black Client." *American Journal of Orthopsychiatry.* 40:39-46.

Cantor, M., K. Rosenthal, and L. Wilker.
1975   "Social and Family Relations of Black Aged Women in New York City." *Gerontologist.* 15(5):64.

Caplan, Nathan.
1970   "The New Ghetto Man: A Review of Recent Empirical Studies." *Journal of Social Issues.* 26:59-74.

Caplovitz, David.
1963   *The Poor Pay More: Consumer Practices of Low-Income Families.* New York: Free Press.

Carlinder, Geoffrey.
1975   "Determinants of Household Hardship." *Journal of Marriage and the Family.* 37:28-38.

Carper, Laura.
1966   "The Negro Family and the Moynihan Report." *Dissent.*
        13:133-140.
Carter, Hugh, and Paul C. Glick.
1970   *Marriage and Divorce: A Social and Economic Study.* Cambridge,
        Mass.: Harvard University Press.
Carter, James H.
1972   "The Black Struggle for Identity." *Journal of the National Medical
        Association.* 64:236-238, 249.
Carter, Louis F.
1968   "Racial Caste Hypogamy: A Sociological Myth?" *Phylon.*
        29:347-350.
Carter-Saltzman, Louise, Sandra Scarr-Salapatek, and William B. Barker.
1975   "Do These Co-Twins Really Live Together? An Assessment of
        the Validity of the Home Index as a Measure of Family
        Socio-Economic Status." *Educational and Psychological Measure-
        ment.* 35(2):427-435.
Cavan, Ruth Shonle.
1959   "Negro Family Disorganization and Juvenile Delinquency."
        Journal of Negro Education. 28:230-239.
Cazenave, Noel A.
1979   "Middle Income Black Fathers—Analysis of the Provider Role."
        Family Coordinator. 28(4):583-593.
Chemezie, Amuzie.
1975   "Transracial Adoption of Black Children." *Social Work.*
        20(4):296-301.
1976   "Black Identity and the Grow-Shapiro Study on Trans-racial
        Adoption." *The Journal of Afro-American Issues.* 4:139-152.
Chestang, Leon.
1972   "The Dilemma of Biracial Adoption." *Social Work.* 17:100-105.
Chilman, Catherine S.
1965   "Child Rearing and Family Relationship Patterns of the Very
        Poor." *Welfare in Review.* 3:9-19.
1966a   "Comment on Bernard." *Journal of Marriage and the Family.*
        28:446-448.
1966b   *Growing Up Poor.* Department of Health, Education and Welfare,
        Welfare Administration Publication No. 13. Washington, D.C.:
        U.S. Government Printing Office.
1975   "Families in Poverty in the Early 1970's: Rates, Associated
        Factors, Some Implications." *Journal of Marriage and the Family.*
        37(1):49-60.

Chilman, Catherine S., and Marvin B. Sussman.
1964   "Poverty in the United States in the Mid-Sixties." *Journal of Marriage and the Family.* 26:391-395.

Christensen, Harold T.
1960   "Cultural Relativism and Premarital Sex Norms." *American Sociological Review.* 25:31-39.

1964   ed., *Handbook of Marriage and the Family.* Chicago: Rand McNally.

Christensen, Harold T., and Leanor B. Johnson.
1978   "Premarital Coitus and the Southern Black: A Comparative View." *Journal of Marriage and the Family.* 40:721-732.

Christenson, James A., and Choon Yang.
1976   "Dominant Value in American Society: An Exploratory Analysis." *Sociology and Social Research.* 60:461-473.

Christmas, June J.
1969   "Sociopsychiatric Rehabilitation in a Black Urban Ghetto: Conflicts, Issues, and Directions." *American Journal of Orthopsychiatry.* 39:651-661.

1973   "Psychological Stresses of Urban Living: New Directions for Mental Health Services in the Inner City." *Journal of the National Medical Association.* 65:483-486, 511.

Clark, Candace.
1977   "Abortion Predisposition and Behavior Among Black and White Mothers." *Population Index.* 43(3):422-423.

Clark, Kenneth.
1965   *Dark Ghetto.* New York: Harper and Row.

Clarke, J. W.
1973   "Family Structure and Political Socialization Among Urban Black Children." *American Journal of Political Science.* 17:302-315.

Clemente, Fraud, and William J. Sauer.
1976   "Racial Differences in Life Satisfaction." *Journal of Black Studies.* 7(1):3-10.

Cohen, Albert K., and Harold Hodges.
1963   "Characteristics of the Lower Blue Collar Class." *Social Problems.* 10:303-334.

Coleman, James.
1966   *Equality of Educational Opportunity.* Washington, D.C.: U.S. Department of Health, Education and Welfare, Office of Education.

Coles, Robert.
1963   "Racial Identity in School Children." *Saturday Review.* 46: 56-57, 68-69.

1965   "It's the Same, But It's Different." *Daedalus*. 94:1107-1132.

1967   *Children of Crisis: A Study of Courage and Fear*. Boston: Little Brown.

Comer, James P.

1972   *Beyond Black and White*. New York: Quadrangle Books.

1974   "Black Children In A Racist Society." *Current*. 162:53-56.

Copeland, Elaine J.

1977   "Counseling Black Women with Negative Self-Concepts." *Personnel and Guidance Journal*. 55:397-400.

Copeland, Lewis C.

1939   "The Negro as a Contrast Conception." In Edgar T. Thompson, ed., *Race Relations and the Race Problem*. Durham, N.C.: Duke University Press.

Corkey, Elizabeth C.

1964   "A Family Planning Program for the Low-Income Family." *Journal of Marriage and the Family*. 26:478-480.

Cornely, Paul B.

1970   "Community Participation and Control: A Possible Answer to Racism in Health." *Milbank Memorial Fund Quarterly*. 48:347-362.

Cortes, C., and E. Fleming.

1968   "The Effects of Father Absence on the Adjustment of Culturally Disadvantaged Boys." *Journal of Special Education*. 2:413-420.

Cosby, Arthur.

1971   "Black-White Differences in Aspirations Among Deep South High School Students." *Journal of Negro Education*. 40:17-21.

Coser, Lewis A.

1965   "The Sociology of Poverty." *Social Problems*. 13:140-148.

1971   *Masters of Sociological Thought*. New York: Harcourt Brace Jovanovich.

Coser, Lewis A., and Bernard Rosenberg.

1969   *Sociological Theory: A Book of Readings*. New York: Macmillan.

Cottle, Thomas J.

1974   *Black Children, White Dreams*. Boston: Houghton Mifflin.

Counter, Alan.

1977   "In Search of the Bush Afro-American." Symposium. University of California, Berkeley. May 1977.

Cox, Oliver C.

1940   "Sex Ratios and Marital Status Among Negroes." *American Sociological Review*. 5:937-941.

1948   *Caste, Class and Race*. New York: Doubleday and Company.

1976   *Race Relations: Elements and Social Dynamics*. Detroit: Wayne State University Press.

Cromwell, Vicky L., and Ronald E. Cromwell.

1978   "Perceived Dominance in Decision Making and Conflict Resolution Among Anglo, Black and Chicano Couples." *Journal of Marriage and the Family*. 40(4):749-759.

Cummings, Scott.

1977   "Family Socialization and Fatalism Among Black Adolescents." *Journal of Negro Education*. 46(1):62-75.

Curtis, Russel L., Jr., and Louis A. Zurcher, Jr.

1971   "Voluntary Associations and the Social Integration of the Poor." *Social Problems*. 18:339-357.

Dai, B.

1953   "Some Problems of Personality Development Among Negro Children." In C. Kluckholn, H. A. Murray, and D. M. Schneider, eds., *Personality in Nature, Society and Culture*. New York: Knopf. Pages 545-566.

Darity, William.

1975   "Economic Theory and Racial Economic Inequality." *Review of Black Political Economy*. 5:225-248.

Darity, William, and Castellano Turner.

1978   "Family Planning, Race Consciousness, and the Fear of Racial Genocide." In Robert Staples, ed., *The Black Family: Essays and Studies*. Second edition. Belmont, Calif.: Wadsworth.

Datesman, Susan K., and Frank R. Scarpitti.

1975   "Female Delinquency and Broken Homes: A Reassessment." *Criminology*. 13(1):33-55.

Davis, Allison.

1965   *Deep South: A Social Anthropological Study of Caste and Class*. Chicago: University of Chicago Press.

Davis, Allison, and John Dollard.

1940   *Children of Bondage: The Personality Development of Negro Youth in the Urban South*. Washington, D.C.: American Council on Education.

Davis, Allison, and Robert J. Havighurst.

1946   "Social Class and Color Differences in Child Rearing." *American Sociological Review*. 11:698-710.

1947   *The Father of the Man: How Your Child Gets His Personality*. Boston: Houghton Mifflin.

Davis, Angela.

1971   "Reflections on the Black Woman's Role in the Community of Slaves." *The Black Scholar*. 3:2-15.

Davis, Elizabeth B.
1968   "The American Negro: From Family Membership to Personal and Societal Identity." *Journal of the National Medical Association.* 60:72-79.

Davis, Frank G.
1972   *The Economics of Black Community Development.* Chicago: Markham Publishing Company.

Davis, George A., and O. Fred Donaldson.
1975   *Blacks in the United States: A Geographic Perspective.* Boston: Houghton Mifflin.

Day, C. B., and E. A. Hooton.
1932   *A Study of Some Negro and White Families in the United States.* Cambridge: Peabody Museum, Harvard University.

de Almeida [Engram], Eleanor.
1977   "Whose Values? Racial Chauvinism in Research on Black Families." *The Black Sociologist.* 6(1):9-24.

Deasy, Leila Calhoun, and Olive Westbrooke Quinn.
1962   "The Urban Negro and Adoption of Children." *Child Welfare.* 41:400-410.

Degler, Carl N.
1971   *Neither Blacks Nor White.* New York: Macmillan.

Dennis, R. M.
1976   "Theories of the Black Family: The Weak Family and Strong Family Schools as Competing Ideologies." *Journal of Afro-American Issues.* 4:315-328.

Derbyshire, R. L., and E. B. Brody.
1964   "Marginality Identity and Behavior in the Negro: A Functional Analysis." *The International Journal of Social Psychiatry.* 10:7-13.

Derbyshire, R. L., et al.
1963   "Family Structure of Young Adult Negro Male Patients: Preliminary Observations from Urban Baltimore." *Journal of Nervous and Mental Disease.* 136:245-251.

Derbyshire, Robert L., and Sata Lindberg.
1968   "From Slum to Asylum: A Selective Process." *Mental Hygiene.* 52:542-547.

DiAngi, Paulette.
1976   "Erickson's Theory of Personality Development as Applied to the Black Child." *Perspectives in Psychiatric Care.* 14(4):184-185.

Dickinson, George E.
1975   "Dating Behavior of Black and White Adolescents Before and After Desegregation." *Journal of Marriage and the Family.* 37:602-608.

Dietrich, Kathryn Thomas.
1975   "A Reexamination of the Myth of Black Matriarchy." *Journal of Marriage and the Family*. 37:367-374.

Diggs, Mary H.
1950   "Some Problems and Needs of Negro Children as Revealed by Comparative Delinquency and Crime Statistics." *Journal of Negro Education*. 19:290-297.

Dill, Bonnie Thornton.
1975   "The Dialectics of Black Womanhood: Towards a New Model of American Femininity." Unpublished Paper. Presented to the American Sociological Association. August.

Dillard, John M.
1976   "Relationship Between Career Maturity and Self-Concepts of Suburban and Urban Middle- and Urban Lower-Class Pre-adolescent Black Males." *Journal of Vocational Behavior*. 9(3): 311-320.

Donald, Henderson H.
1952   *The Negro Freedman*. New York: Henry Schoman.

Donohue, Thomas R.
1975   "Effect of Commercials on Black Children." *Journal of Advertising Research*. 15(6):41-47.

Dougherty, Molly C.
1978   *Becoming a Woman in Rural Black Culture*. Nashville, Tenn.: Vanderbilt University Press.

Douglass, Joseph H.
1966   "The Urban Negro Family." In John P. Davis, ed., *American Negro Reference Book*. Englewood Cliffs, N.J.: Prentice-Hall.

Dowd, J. J., and V. I. Bengston.
1975   "Social Participation, Age and Ethnicity: An Examination of the 'Double Jeopardy' Hypothesis." *Gerontologist*. 15(5):63.

Dowdall, George W.
1977   "Intermetropolitan Differences in Family Income Inequality: An Ecological Analysis of Total White and Non-White Patterns in 1960." *Sociology and Social Research*. 61(2):176-191.

Drake, St. Clair.
1965   "The Social and Economic Status of the Negro in the United States." *Daedalus*. 44:771-814.

Drake, St. Clair, and Horace Cayton.
1945   *Black Metropolis: A Study of Negro Life in a Northern City*. New York: Harcourt, Brace and Company.

Du Bois, W. E. B.
1899   *The Philadelphia Negro*. Philadelphia: University of Pennsylvania Press.

1909   *The Negro American Family*. Cambridge, Mass.: M.I.T. Press.

1961   *The Souls of Black Folk*. New York: Premier Edition. Originally published in 1903.

Duncan, Beverly, and Otis Dudley Duncan.

1968   "Minorities and the Process of Stratification." *American Sociological Review*. 33:356-364.

1969   "Family Stability and Occupational Success." *Social Problems*. 16:273-285.

Dunkle, Ruth E.

1975   "Racial Differences in the Confidant Relationship." *Gerontologist*. 15(5):74.

Dunmore, Charlotte J.

1976   *Black Children and Their Families: A Bibliography*. San Francisco: R & E Research Associates.

Durrett, Mary Ellen, Shirley O'Bryant, and James W. Pennebaker.

1975   "Child Rearing Reports of White, Black, and Mexican-American." *Developmental Psychology*. 11(6):871.

Dyer, William G.

1964   "Family Reactions to the Fathers' Job." In A. B. Shostak and W. Gombar, eds., *Blue-Collar World*. Englewood Cliffs, N.J.: Prentice-Hall.

Earl, Lovelene, and Nancy Lohmann.

1978   "Absent Fathers and Black Male Children." *Social Work*. 23(5):413-415.

Edwards, G. Franklin.

1953   "Marital Status and General Family Characteristics of the Non-White Population." *Journal of Negro Education*. 22:280-296.

1959   ed., *The Negro Professional Class*. Glencoe, Ill.: Free Press.

1963   "Marriage and Family Life Among Negroes." *Journal of Negro Education*. 32:451-465.

1966   "Community and Class Realities: The Ordeal of Change." *Daedalus*. 95:1-23.

1968   ed., *E. Franklin Frazier on Race Relations*. Chicago: University of Chicago Press.

Edwards, Harry.

1968   "Black Muslim and Negro Christian Family Relationships." *Journal of Marriage and the Family*. 30:604-611.

Eggleston, Cecelia.

1938   "What a Negro Mother Faces." *Forum*. 100:59-62.

Elder, Glenn H., Jr.

1969   "Appearance and Education in Marriage Mobility." *American Sociological Review*. 34:519-533.

1974   *Children of the Great Depression.* Chicago: University of Chicago Press.

Elkins, Stanley M.
1968   *Slavery.* Chicago: University of Chicago Press.

Emerson, Robert, and Martin Kilson.
1965   "The American Dilemma in a Changing World: The Rise of Africa and the Negro American." *Daedalus.* 94:1055-1084.

Endo, Russell.
1973   *Perspectives on Black Americans.* Englewood Cliffs, N.J.: Prentice-Hall.

English, Richard H.
1974   "Beyond Pathology: Research and Theoretical Perspectives on Black Families." In Lawrence E. Gary, ed., *Social Research and the Black Community: Selected Issues and Priorities.* Washington, D.C.: Howard University, Institute for Urban Affairs and Research. Pages 53-65.

Engram, Eleanor [de Almeida].
1977   "Whose Values? Racial Chauvinism in Research on Black Families." *The Black Sociologist.* 6(1):9-24.
1980   "Role Transition in Early Adulthood: Orientations of Young Black Women." In LaFrances Rodgers-Rose, ed., *The Black Woman.* Beverly Hills, Calif.: Sage. Pages 175-187.

Epstein, Ralph, and S. S. Komorita.
1966   "Prejudice Among Negro Children as Related to Parental Ethnocentrism and Punitiveness." *Journal of Personality and Social Psychology.* 4:643-647.

Ericksen, Julia A.
1977   "An Analysis of the Journey to Work for Women." *Social Problems.* 24(4):428-435.

Erickson, E.
1966   "The Concept of Identity in Race Relations: Notes and Queries." In T. Parsons and K. Clark, eds., *The Negro American.* Boston: Houghton Mifflin.

Erickson, Erik H.
1950   *Childhood and Society.* New York: W. W. Norton and Company.
1964   "Memorandum on Identity and Negro Youth." *Journal of Social Issues.* 20:29-42.
1968   *Identity Youth and Crisis.* New York: W. W. Norton and Company.

Ernhart, Claire B.
1975   "Changes in Authoritarian Family Ideology with Childrearing Experience." *Psychological Reports.* 37(2):567-570.

Eshlerman, J. Ross.
1974   *The Family: An Introduction.* Boston: Allyn and Bacon.

Etzkowitz, Henry, and Gerald M. Schaflander.
1969   *Ghetto Crisis.* Boston: Little, Brown.

Ewer, Phyllis, and James O. Gibbs.
1975   "Relationship with Putative Father and Use of Contraception in a Population of Black Adolescent Mothers." *Public Health Reports.* 90(5):417-423.

Fanshell, David.
1957   *A Study in Negro Adoption.* New York: Child Welfare League of America.

Farber, Bernard.
1964   *Family: Organization and Interaction.* San Francisco: Chandler Publishing Company.

Farley, Reynolds.
1970a   "Fertility Among Urban Blacks." *The Milbank Memorial Fund Quarterly.* 48:183-214.

1970b   *Growth of the Black Population.* Chicago: Markham Publishing Company.

Farley, Reynolds, and Albert I. Hermalin.
1971   "Family Stability: A Comparison of Trends Between Blacks and Whites." *American Sociological Review.* 36:1-17.

Farmer, James.
1968   "The Plight of Negro Children in America Today." *Child Welfare.* 47:508-515.

Farran, Dale C., and Craig T. Ramsey.
1977   "Infant Day Care and Attachment Behaviors Toward Mothers and Teachers." *Child Development.* 48(3):1112-1116.

Fave, L. Richard Della.
1974   "The Culture of Poverty Revisited: A Strategy for Research." *Social Problems.* 21(5):609-620.

Feagin, Joe R.
1969   "The Kinship Ties of Negro Urbanites." *Social Science Quarterly.* 49:660-665.

1972   "Black Women in the American Work Force." In Charles V. Willie, ed., *Family Life of Black People.* Columbus, Ohio: Charles E. Merrill.

Feldstein, Stanley.
1971   *Once a Slave: The Slaves' View of Slavery.* New York: William Morrow and Co.

Ferman, Louis A., Joyce L. Kornbluh, and Alan Haber, eds.
1965   *Poverty in America.* Ann Arbor: University of Michigan Press.

Ferman, Louis A., Joyce L. Kornbluh, and J. A. Miller, eds.
1968   *Negroes and Jobs.* Ann Arbor: University of Michigan Press.

Fischer, Ann, Joseph Beasley, and Carl Horter.
1968   "The Occurrence of the Extended Family at the Origin of the Family of Procreation: A Developmental Approach to Negro Family Structure." *Journal of Marriage and the Family.* 30:290-300.

Fisher, Sethand.
1970   *Power and the Black Community: A Reader on Racial Subordination in the United States.* New York: Knopf.

Fogel, Robert W., and Stanley L. Engerman.
1974a   *Time on the Cross: The Economics of American Negro Slavery.* Boston: Little Brown.

1974b   *Time on the Cross: Evidence and Methods.* Boston: Little, Brown.

Foley, Eugene P.
1968   *The Achieving Ghetto.* Washington, D.C.: National Press.

Foley, Vincent D.
1975   "Therapy with Black, Disadvantaged Families: Some Observations on Roles, Communication, and Technique." *Journal of Marriage and Family Counseling.* 1:29-38.

Ford, Beverly O.
1977   "Case Studies of Black Female Heads of Household in the Welfare System: Socialization and Survival." *Western Journal of Black Studies.* 1(2):114-118.

Forman, Robert E.
1971   *Black Ghettos, White Ghettos and Slums.* Englewood Cliffs, N.J.: Prentice-Hall.

Fowler, Irving A.
1966   "The Urban Middle-Class Negro and Adoption: Two Series of Studies and Their Implications for Action." *Child Welfare.* 45:522-525.

Franklin, John Hope.
1952   *From Slavery to Freedom.* New York: Knopf.

Frazier, E. Franklin.
1930   "The Negro Slave Family." *Journal of Negro History.* 15: 198-259.

1932a   "An Analysis of Statistics on Negro Illegitimacy in the United States." *Social Forces.* 11:249-257.

1932b   *The Free Negro Family.* Nashville, Tenn.: Fisk University Press.

1932c   *The Negro Family in Chicago.* Chicago: University of Chicago Press.

1937a   "The Impact of Urban Civilization Upon Negro Family Life." *American Sociological Review.* 2:609-618.

1937b   "Negro Harlem: An Ecological Study." *American Journal of Sociology.* 43:72-88.

1938   "Some Effects of the Depression on the Negro in Northern Cities." *Science and Society*. 2:489-499.

1939   *The Negro Family in the United States*. Chicago: University of Chicago Press.

1940   *Negro Youth at the Crossways*. New York: Schocken Books. Introduction by St. Clair Drake, 1967.

1948   "Ethnic Family Patterns: The Negro Family in the United States." *American Journal of Sociology*. 53:435-438.

1950   "Problems and Needs of Negro Children and Youth Resulting from Family Disorganization." *Journal of Negro Education*. 19:269-277.

1957   *Black Bourgeoisie*. Glencoe, Ill.: Free Press.

1961   "Negro Sex Life of the African and American." In Albert Ellis and Albert Arbanel, eds., *The Encyclopedia of Sexual Behavior*. New York: Hawthorne Books.

1962   "The Failure of the Negro Intellectual." *Negro Digest*. 30: 214-222.

1964   "The Negro Family in Chicago." In E. W. Burgess and D. J. Bogue, eds., *Contributions to Urban Sociology*. Chicago: University of Chicago Press. Pages 404-418.

Fredericks, Marcel A., and Paul Mundy.

1977   "Models for Teaching Health Care Professionals the Components of the Family." *National Medical Association Journal*. 69:343-347.

Frumkin, Robert M.

1954   "Attitudes of Negro College Students Toward Intrafamily Leadership and Control." *Marriage and Family Living*. 16:252-253.

Furnas, J. C.

1956   *Goodbye to Uncle Tom*. New York: William Sloane Associates.

Furstenberg, Frank F.

1970   "Premarital Pregnancy Among Black Teenagers." *Transaction*. 7:52-55.

1972   "Attitudes Toward Abortion Among Young Blacks." *Studies in Family Planning*. 3:66-69.

1976   *Unplanned Parenthood*. Glencoe, Ill.: Free Press.

Gans, Herbert.

1962   *The Urban Villagers*. Glencoe, Ill.: Free Press.

1965   "The Negro Family: Reflections on the Moynihan Report." *Commonwealth*. 83:47-51.

Garcia, Claudia, and Hanna Levenson.

1975   "Differences Between Blacks' and Whites' Expectations of Control by Chance and Powerful Others." *Psychological Reports*. 37(2):563-566.

Garrett, Gerald R., and Howard M. Bahr.
1976   "The Family Backgrounds of Skid Row Women," *Signs: Journal of Women in Culture and Society.* 2(2)369-381.

Gary, Lawrence, ed.
1974   *Social Research in the Black Community: Selected Issues and Priorities.* Washington, D.C.: Institute for Urban Affairs and Research.

Gebhard, Paul, et al.
1958   *Pregnancy, Birth and Abortion.* New York: Harper and Brothers.

Geer, Michael, and Walter R. Gove.
1974   "Race, Sex and Marital Status: Their Effect on Mortality." *Social Problems.* 21:567-579.

Geismar, Ludwig.
1968   "Social Class, Ethnicity, and Family Functioning: Exploring Some Issues Raised by the Moynihan Report." *Journal of Marriage and the Family.* 30:480-487.

Geismar, Ludwig, et al.
1962   "Measuring Family Disorganization." *Marriage and Family Living.* 24:51-56.

Genovese, Eugene.
1974a   *Roll Jordan Roll: The World the Slaves Made.* New York: Pantheon.
1974b   "The Slave Family, Woman—A Reassessment of Matriarchy, Emasculation, Weakness." *Southern Workman.* 1.

Gilman, Richard, and David Knox.
1976   "Coping with Fatherhood: The First Year." *Child Psychiatry and Human Development.* 6(3):134-148.

Glantz, Oscar.
1976   "Family Structure, Fate Control and Counter-Normative Political Beliefs Among Lower-Class Black Students." *College Student Journal.* 10(2):121-126.

Glasser, Paul H., and Lois N. Glasser.
1970   *Families in Crisis.* New York: Harper and Row.

Glazer, Nathan, and Daniel P. Moynihan.
1970   *Beyond the Melting Pot.* Second edition. Cambridge, Mass.: M.I.T. Press.

Glazer, Nona Y., and Carol F. Creedon, eds.
1968   *Children and Poverty.* Chicago: Rand McNally.

Glick, Paul C.
1970   "Marriage and Marital Stability Among Blacks." *Milbank Memorial Fund Quarterly.* 48 (Part II):98-116.

Glick, Paul C., and Arthur Norton.
1971   "Frequency, Duration and Probability of Marriage and Divorce." *Journal of Marriage and the Family.* 33:307-316.

Glueck, Eleanor, and Sheldon Glueck.
1957   "Working Mothers and Delinquency." *Mental Hygiene.* 41: 327-352.

Gold, M. A.
1961   *A Social Psychology of Delinquent Boys.* Ann Arbor, Mich.: Institute for Social Research.

Goldschmid, Marcel L., ed.
1970   *Black Americans and White Racism.* New York: Holt, Rinehart and Winston.

Goldstein, Gerard.
1971   *Low Income Youth in Urban Areas: A Critical Review of the Literature.* New York: Holt, Rinehart and Winston.

Goldstein, Rhoda L., ed.
1971   *Black Life and Culture in the United States.* New York: Thomas Y. Crowell.

Goode, William J.
1951   "Economic Factors and Marital Stability." *American Sociological Review.* 16:802-812.

1956   *After Divorce.* New York: Free Press.

1960   "Illegitimacy in the Caribbean Social Structure." *American Sociological Review.* 25:21-30.

1962   *World Revolution and Family Patterns.* Glencoe, Ill.: Free Press.

1964   *The Family.* Englewood Cliffs, N.J.: Prentice-Hall.

Gouldner, Alvin W.
1962   "Anti-Minotaur: The Myth of a Value-Free Sociology." *Social Problems.* 9:199-213.

Grier, W. H.
1966   "Some Special Effects of Negroeness on the Oedipal Conflict." *Journal of the National Medical Association.* 58:416-418.

Grier, William, and Price Cobbs.
1968   *Black Rage.* New York: Basic Books.

Grindereng, Margaret P.
1976   "Families Behind the AFDC. Stereotype." *Journal of Extension.* 14:8-15.

Grow, Lucille J., and Deborah Shapiro.
1975a   "Adoption of Black Children by White Parents." *Child Welfare.* 54(1):57-59.

1975b   *Black Children, White Parents: A Study of Transracial Adoption.* New York: Child Welfare League of America.

Gump, Janice Porter.
1975   "Comparative Analysis of Black Women's and White Women's Sex-Role Attitudes." *Journal of Consulting and Clinical Psychology.* 43(6):585-563.

Gurin, Patricia, and Edgar G. Epps.
1975   *Black Consciousness, Identity and Achievement: A Study of Students in Historically Black Colleges.* New York: John Wiley and Sons.

Guterman, Stanley S.
1972   *Black Psyche: The Modal Personality Patterns of Black Americans.* Berkeley, Calif.: Glendessary Press.

Gutman, Herbert G.
1975   *Slavery and the Numbers Game: A Critique of Time on the Cross.* Urbana, Ill.: University of Illinois Press.
1976a   *The Black Family in Slavery and Freedom, 1750-1925.* New York: Pantheon.
1976b   "A New Look at Black Families and Slavery." *Current.* 188:3-9.

Hage, Jerald.
1972   *Techniques and Problems of Theory Construction in Sociology.* New York: John Wiley and Sons.

Haley, Alex.
1976   *Roots: The Saga of an American Family.* New York: Doubleday and Co.

Hallow, Ralph Z.
1969   "The Blacks Cry Genocide." *Nation.* 208:535-537.

Hammond, Boone, and Joyce Ladner.
1969   "Socialization into Sexual Behavior in a Negro Slum Ghetto." In Carlfred Broderick and Jessie Bernard, eds., *The Individual, Sex and Society.* Baltimore: Johns Hopkins University Press.

Hammond, Judith, and J. Rex Enoch.
1976   "Conjugal Power Relations Among Black Working-Class Families." *Journal of Black Studies.* 7(1):107-123.

Hampton, R. C.
1979   "Husbands' Characteristics and Marital Disruption in Black Families." *Sociological Quarterly.* 20(2):255-266.

Hand, H. B.
1975   "Working Mothers and Maladjusted Children." *Journal of Educational Sociology.* 30:245-246.

Haney, C. Allen, et al.
1975   "Characteristics of Black Women in Male and Female Headed Households." *Journal of Black Studies.* 6:136-157.

Hannerz, Ulf.
1969a   "Roots of Black Manhood." *Transaction.* 6:12-21.
1969b   *Soulside: Inquiries into Ghetto Culture and Community.* New York: Columbia University Press.
1970   "What Ghetto Males Are Like: Another Look." In Norman E. Whitten and John F. Szwed, eds., *Afro-American Anthropology.* New York: Free Press.

Hansen, Niles M.

1970   *Rural Poverty and the Urban Crisis.* Bloomington: Indiana University Press.

Hare, Bruce R.

1977   "Black and White Child Self-Esteem in Social Science: An Overview." *Journal of Negro Education.* 46(2):141-156.

Hare, Nathan.

1964   "The Frustrated Masculinity of the Negro Male." *Negro Digest.* 13:5-9.

1965a   *Black Anglo-Saxons.* New York: Marzone and Munsell.

1965b   "Recent Trends in the Occupational Mobility of Negroes 1930-1960: An Intracohort Analysis." *Social Forces.* 44:166-173.

1973   "Challenge of a Black Scholar." In Joyce A. Ladner, ed., *The Death of White Sociology.* New York: Random House.

1976   "What Black Intellectuals Misunderstand about the Black Family." *Black World.* 25:4-14.

Harrell-Bond, Barbara E.

1976   "Stereotypes of Western and African Patterns of Marriage and Family Life." *Journal of Marriage and the Family.* 38:387-396.

Harrington, Michael.

1962   *The Other America: Poverty in the United States.* New York: Macmillan.

Harris, Marvin.

1975   *Culture, People, Nature.* New York: Thomas Y. Crowell.

Harris, W.

1976   "Work and Family in Black Atlanta, 1880." *Journal of Social History.* 9(3):319-330.

Harrison, Algea O.

1974   "Dilemma of Growing Up Black and Female." *Journal of Social and Behavioral Sciences.* 20:28-40.

Harrison, Danny E., Walter H. Bennett, and Gerald Globetti.

1969   "Attitudes of Rural Youth Toward Premarital Sexual Permissiveness." *Journal of Marriage and the Family.* 31:783-787.

Harrison, Robert H., and Edward H. Kass.

1967   "Differences Between Negro and White Pregnant Women on the MMPI." *Journal of Consulting Psychology.* 31:454-463.

Harrison-Ross, Phillis, and Barbara Wyden.

1973   *The Black Child A Parent's Guide.* New York: Peter H. Wyden.

Hartnagel, Timothy F.

1970   "Father Absence and Self Conception Among Lower Class White and Negro Boys." *Social Problems.* 18:152-163.

Harwood, E., and C. Hodge.
1971   "Jobs and the Negro Family: A Reappraisal." *The Public Interest.* 23:125-131.

Hauser, Philip M.
1965   "Demographic Factors in the Integration of the Negro." *Daedalus.* 94:847-877.

Hawkins, H. C.
1976   "Urban Housing and the Black Family." *Phylon.* 37(1):73-84.

Hawkins, Mildred.
1960   "Negro Adoptions—Challenge Accepted." *Child Welfare.* 39(10): 22-27.

Haynes, George E.
1924   "Negro Migration: Its Effect On Family and Community Life in the North." *Opportunity.* 1:271-274, 303-306.

Hays, William C., and Charles H. Mindel.
1973   "Extended Kinship Relations in Black and White Families." *Journal of Marriage and the Family.* 35:51-52.
1977   "Parental Perceptions for Children: A Comparison of Black and White Families." *Ethnic Groups.* 1(4):281-295.

Heer, David M.
1958   "Dominance and the Working Wife." *Social Forces.* 30:341-347.
1963   "The Measurement and Bases of Family Power: An Overview." *Marriage and Family Living.* 25:133-139.
1966   "Negro-White Marriage in the United States." *Journal of Marriage and the Family.* 28:262-273.

Heiss, Jerald.
1972   "On the Transmission of Marital Instability in Black Families." *American Sociological Review.* 37:82-92.
1975   *The Case of the Black Family: A Sociological Inquiry.* New York: Columbia University Press.

Helzer, John E.
1975   "Bipolar Affective Disorder in Black and White Men: A Comparison of Symptoms and Familial Illness." *Archives of General Psychiatry.* 32(9):1140-1143.

Hendin, Herbert.
1969   *Black Suicide.* New York: Basic Books.

Henri, Florette.
1976   *Black Migration: Movement North 1900-1920.* Garden City, N.Y.: Anchor Books.

Henriques, Fernando.
1975   *Children of Conflict.* New York: E.P. Dutton and Company.

Henry, J., and J. Bogg.

1952   "Child Rearing, Culture and the Natural World." *Psychiatry.* 15:261-271.

Hernton, Calvin.

1965   *Sex and Racism in America.* New York: Doubleday and Company.

Herschberg, Theodore.

1972   "Free Blacks in Antebellum Philadelphia: A Study of Ex-Slaves, Freeborn, and Socio-economic Decline." *Journal of Social History.* 5:183-209.

Herskovits, Melville J.

1928   *The American Negro.* New York: Harper and Brothers.

1933   "On the Provenance of New World Negroes." *Social Forces.* 12:252-259.

1958   *The Myth of the Negro Past.* Boston: Beacon Press.

Herson, Jay, Cyril L. Crocker, and Ernest Butts.

1975   "Comprehensive Family Planning Services to an Urban Black Community: A Three Year Experience." *Journal of the National Medical Association.* 67(1):61-65.

Herta, Hilda, and Sue Warren Little.

1944   "Unmarried Negro Mothers in a Southern Urban Community." *Social Forces.* 23:73-79.

Herzog, Elizabeth.

1962   "Unmarried Mothers: Some Questions to Be Answered, and Some Answers to Be Questioned." *Child Welfare.* 41:339-350.

1966   "Is There a 'Breakdown' of the Negro Family?" *Social Work.* 11:3-10.

Herzog, Elizabeth, and Rose Bernstein.

1965   "Why So Few Negro Adoptions?" *Children.* 12:14-18.

Herzog, Elizabeth, and Hylan Lewis.

1970   "Children in Poor Families: Myths and Realities." *American Journal of Orthopsychiatry.* 40:375-385.

Herzog, Elizabeth, and Cecelia E. Sudia.

1969   "Family Structure and Composition." In Roger R. Miller, ed., *Race, Research, and Reason: Social Work Perspectives.* New York: National Association of Social Workers. Pages 145-164.

1970   *Boys in Fatherless Families.* U.S. Department of Health, Education and Welfare, Office of Child Development, Children's Bureau. Washington, D.C.: U.S. Government Printing Office.

Herzog, Elizabeth, Cecelia Sudia, Jane Harwood, and Carol Newcomb.

1969   *Families for Black Children: The Search for Adoptive Parents.* A

Cooperative Report of the Division of Research and Evaluation. Washington, D.C.: George Washington University.

Hetherington, E. Mavis.

1965   "A Developmental Study of the Effects of Sex of the Dominant Parent on Sex Role Preference, Identification, and Imitation in Children." *Journal of Personality and Social Psychology.* 2:188-194.

1966   "Effects of Paternal Absence on Sex-Typed Behaviors in Negro and White Pre-Adolescent Males." *Journal of Personality and Social Psychology.* 4:87-91.

Hetherington, M., and J. Deur.

1971   "The Effects of Father-Absence on Child Development." *Young Children.* 26:233-244.

Hiday, Virginia A.

1975   "Parity and Well-Being Among Low-Income Urban Families." *Journal of Marriage and the Family.* 37(4):789-797.

Hill, Adelaide Cromwell, and Frederick S. Jaffe.

1967   "Negro Fertility and Family Size Preferences: Implications for Programming of Health and Social Services." In Talcott Parsons and Kenneth B. Clark, eds., *The Negro American.* Boston: Beacon Press.

Hill, Herbert.

1976   "Of Blacks and Whites and Family Stability." *Current.* 188:11-12.

Hill, Mozell C.

1957   "Research on the Negro Family." *Marriage and Family Living.* 19:25-31.

Hill, Reuben, and Donald A. Hansen.

1960   "The Identification of Conceptual Frameworks Utilized in Family Study." *Marriage and Family Living.* 22:299-311.

Hill, Robert B.

1972   *The Strengths of Black Families.* New York: Emerson Hall.

1975   *Black Families in the 1974-75 Depression: Policy Report.* New York: National Urban League.

1977   *Informal Adoption Among Black Families.* Washington, D.C.: National Urban League Research Department.

1978   "Building on Our Strengths." *Carleton Voice.* 43(2):18-20.

Hill, Robert B., and L. Shaclef.

1975   "Black Extended Family Revisited." *Urban League Review.* 1(2):18-24.

Hill, Rodman.

1977   "Family Therapy Workshop: When the Family and the Therapist are of Different Races." *Journal of Contemporary Psychotherapy.* 9(1):45-46.

Himes, Joseph S.
1954   "A Value Profile in Mate Selection Among Negroes." *Marriage and Family Living.* 16:244-247.
1960   "Interrelation of Occupational and Spousal Roles in a Middle-Class Negro Neighborhood." *Marriage and Family Living.* 22: 362-363.
1964a   "Some Reactions to a Hypothetical Premarital Pregnancy by 100 Negro College Women." *Marriage and Family Living.* 26: 344-347.
1964b   "Some Related Cultural Deprivations in Lower Class Negro Youth." *Journal of Marriage and the Family.* 26:447-451.
Himes, Joseph S., and R. E. Edwards.
1950   "Hair Texture and Skin Color in Mate Selection Among Negroes." *Midwest Journal.* 4:80-85.
Hindelang, Michael James.
1970   "Educational and Occupational Aspirations Among Working Class Negroes, Mexican-Americans and White Elementary School Children." *Journal of Negro Education.* 39:351-353.
Hirschi, Travis, and Hanan C. Selvin.
1972   *Techniques of Survey Analysis.* New York: Free Press.
Hitchcock, Alice E.
1959   "The Relationship Between Maternal Employment and Dependent Behavior Observed in Kindergarten Boys." *Child Development.* 30:533-546.
Hobbs, Daniel F., Jr., and Jane Maynard Wimbish.
1977   "Transition to Parenthood by Black Couples." *Journal of Marriage and the Family.* 39:677-689.
Hofferth, Sandra L.
1979   "Early Childbearing and Later Economic Well-Being." *American Sociological Review.* 44(5):784-815.
Hoffman, Lois W.
1963   "Mother's Enjoyment of Work and Effects on the Child." In F. Ivan Nye and Lois W. Hoffman, eds., *The Employed Mother in America.* Chicago: Rand McNally.
Hollingshead, August B.
1949   *Elmstown's Youth.* New York: John Wiley and Sons.
Howard, Alicia, David D. Royse, and John A. Skerl.
1977   "Transracial Adoption: The Black Community Perspective." *Social Work.* 22(3):184-189.
Hsu, Francis L. K.
1979   "Roots of the American Family: From Noah to Now." In Allan J. Lichtman and Joan R. Challinor, eds., *Kin and*

Communities. Washington, D.C.: Smithsonian Institution Press.

Huggins, Nathan I., M. Kilson, and D. M. Fox, eds.
1971   *Key Issues in the Afro-American Experience.* New York: Harcourt Brace Jovanovich.

Hunt, Janet G., and Larry L. Hunt.
1975a   "Race and the Father-Son Connection: The Conditional Relevance of Father Absence for Orientations and Identities of Adolescent Boys." *Social Problems.* 23(1):35-52.
1975b   "The Sexual Mystique: A Common Dimension of Racial and Sexual Stratification." *Sociology and Social Research.* 59(3):231-242.
1977a   "Race, Daughters and Father-Loss: Does Absence Make the Girl Grow Stronger?" *Social Problems.* 25(1):90-102.
1977b   "Race Father Identification, and Achievement Orientation: The Subjective Side of the Father-Son Connection, A Research Note." *Youth and Society.* 9(1):113-120.

Hyman, Herbert H., and John Shelton Reed.
1969   "Black Matriarchy Reconsidered: Evidence from Secondary Analysis of Sample Surveys." *Public Opinion Quarterly.* 33: 346-354.

Iscoe, Ira, Martha Williams, and Jerry Harvey.
1964   "Age, Intelligence, and Sex as Variables in the Conformity Behavior of Negro and White Children." *Child Development.* 35:451-460.

Jackson, Jacqueline J.
1971   "But Where Are the Men?" *Black Scholar.* 3:30-41.
1973   "Family Organization and Ideology." In R. M. Dreger and K. S. Miller, eds., *Comparative Studies of Negroes and Whites in the United States 1966-1970.* New York: Seminar Press.
1974   "Ordinary Black Husbands: The Truly Hidden Man." *Journal of Social and Behavioral Sciences.* 20:19-27.

Jacques, Jeffrey M.
1976   "Self-Esteem Among Southeastern Black-American Couples." *Journal of Black Studies.* 7:11-28.

James, W. F. Bernell; Pauline M. James, and Edgar Walker.
1977   "Some Problems of Sexual Growth in Adolescent Under-privileged Unwed Black Girls." *Journal of the National Medical Association.* 69(9):631-633.

Jeffers, Camille.
1967   *Living Poor.* Ann Arbor, Mich.: Ann Arbor Publishers.

Jencks, Christopher, et al.
1972   *Inequality.* New York: Harper Colophon.

Johnson, C. Lincoln.
1976   "Transracial Adoption: Victim of Ideology." *Social Work.*
        21(3):241-243.
Johnson, Charles Spurgeon.
1934   *Shadow of the Plantation.* Chicago: University of Chicago Press.
1941   *Growing Up in the Black Belt.* Washington, D.C.: American
        Council on Education.
n.d.   Unpublished manuscript. Atlanta: Atlanta University. Atlanta
        University Archives. Cullen-Jackman Memorial Manuscript
        Collection, Charles Spurgeon Johnson Papers, 1893-1956.
        Charles S. Johnson Collection.
Johnson, Leanor B.
1974   "Relevant Literature in the Study of Black Families: An
        Annotated Bibliography." *Journal of Social and Behavioral Sciences.*
        20:79-100.
1978   "The Sexual Behavior of Southern Blacks." In Robert Staples,
        ed., *The Black Family: Essays and Studies.* Belmont, Calif.:
        Wadsworth. Pages 80-93.
Johnson, Michael P., and Ralph A. Sell.
1976   "The Cost of Being Black: A 1970 Update." *American Journal of
        Sociology.* 82:183-190.
Jones, Rhett.
1973   "Proving Blacks Inferior. The Sociology of Knowledge." In Joyce
        A. Ladner, ed., *The Death of White Sociology.* New York: Random
        House.
Kamii, Constance K., and Norma Radin.
1967   "Class Differences in the Socialization Practices of Negro
        Mothers." *Journal of Marriage and the Family.* 29:302-310.
Kandel, D. P.
1971   "Race, Maternal Authority and Adolescent Aspiration."
        American Journal of Sociology. 76:999-1020.
Kaplan, Abraham.
1964   *The Conduct of Inquiry.* Scranton, Pa.: Chandler Publishing
        Company.
Kardiner, Abram, and Lionel Ovesey.
1951   *The Mark of Oppression.* New York: W. W. Norton and Company.
Karow, B. P.
1958   *The Negro Personality.* New York: Springer.
Kellam, Sheppard G., Margaret E. Ensminger, and R. J. Turner.
1975   "Family Structure and the Mental Health of Children: Concurrent
        and Longitudinal Community-Wide Studies." *Archives of
        General Psychiatry.* 32(9):1012-1022.

Keller, S.
1963   "The Social World of the Urban Slum Child: Some Early Findings." *American Journal of Orthopsychiatry*. 33:823-831.
Kenniston, Kenneth, and the Carnegie Council on Children.
1977   *All Our Children: The American Family Under Pressure*. New York: Harcourt Brace Jovanovich.
Kenyata, Jomo.
1965   *Facing Mount Kenya*. New York: Vintage.
Kephart, William M.
1953   "The Duration of Marriage." *American Sociological Review*. 19:289-295.
1978   *The Family, Society and the Individual*. Third edition. Boston: Houghton Mifflin.
Kephart, William M., and Thomas P. Monahan.
1952   "Desertion and Divorce in Philadelphia?" *American Sociological Review*. 17:719-727.
Kerckhoff, Alan C.
1971   *Educational, Familial, and Peer Group Influences on Occupational Achievement*. Washington, D.C.: U.S. Department of Health, Education and Welfare.
1972   *Socialization and Social Class*. Englewood Cliffs, N.J.: Prentice-Hall.
Kerckhoff, Alan C., and Richard T. Campbell.
1977   "Race and Social Status Differences in the Explanation of Educational Ambition." *Social Forces*. 55(3):701-714.
Kerlinger, Fred N., and Elazur J. Pedhazur.
1973   *Multiple Regression in Behavioral Research*. New York: Holt, Rinehart and Winston.
Kilpatrick, Allie C.
1977   "Future Directions for the Black Family." *Family Coordinator*. 28(3):347-352.
King, C. H.
1967   "Family Therapy with the Deprived Family." *Social Casework*. 48:203-208.
King, Charles E.
1945   "The Negro Maternal Family: A Product of an Economic and a Cultural System." *Social Forces*. 24:100-104.
1954   "The Sex Factor in Marital Adjustment." *Marriage and Family Living*. 16:237-240.
King, James R.
1976   "African Survivals in the Black American Family Key Factors in Stability." *The Journal of Afro-American Issues*. 4:153-167.

King, Karl.
1967   "A Comparison of the Negro and White Family Power Structure in Low-Income Families." *Child and Family*. 6:65-74.
1969   "Adolescent Perception of Power Structure in the Negro Family." *Journal of Marriage and the Family*. 31:751-755.

King, Karl, Thomas J. Abernathy, and Ann H. Chapman.
1976   "Black Adolescents' Views of Maternal Employment as a Threat to the Marital Relationship: 1963-1973." *Journal of Marriage and the Family*. 38(4):733-737.

King, Mae C.
1973   "The Politics of Sexual Stereotypes." *Black Scholar*. 4:12-23.

King, R. J. R.
1969   *Family Relations, Concepts and Theories*. Berkeley: Glendessary Press.

Kirkendall, Lester A.
1961   *Premarital Intercourse and Interpersonal Relationships*. New York: Julian Press.

Kiser, Clyde Vernon.
1969   *Sea Island to City*. New York: Atheneum.

Klotman, Phyllis R.
1978   *The Black Family and the Black Woman: A Bibliography*. New York: Arno.

Kluckhohn, Clyde, H. A. Murray, & D. M. Schneider.
1953   *Personality in Nature, Society and Culture*. New York: Knopf.

Kolb, T. M., and M. A. Straus.
1974   "Marital Power and Marital Happiness in Relation to Problem-Solving Ability," *Journal of Marriage and the Family*. 36:756-766.

Komarovsky, Mirra.
1940   *The Unemployed Man and His Family*. New York: Dryden.
1964   *Blue Collar Marriage*. New York: Random House.

Kriesberg, Louis.
1967   "Rearing Children for Educational Achievement in Fatherless Families." *Journal of Marriage and the Family*. 29:288-301.

Kronus, Sidney.
1970   *The Black Middle-Class*. Columbus, Ohio: Charles E. Merrill Co.

Kunkel, Peter, and Sara Kennard.
1971   *Spout Spring: A Black Community*. Chicago: Rand McNally.

Kunstadter, Peter.
1963   "A Survey of the Consanguine or Matrifocal Family." *American Anthropologist*. 65:56-66.

Kunz, Phillip R., and Merlin B. Brinkerhoff.
1969   "Differential Childlessness by Color: The Destruction of a Cultural Belief." *Journal of Marriage and the Family.* 31:713-719.
Kuvelesky, William P., and A. S. Obodoro.
1972   "A Racial Comparison of Teenage Girls Projections for Marriage and Procreation." *Journal of Marriage and the Family.* 34:75-84.
Ladner, Joyce A.
1972   *Tomorrow's Tomorrow: The Black Woman.* New York: Doubleday Anchor.
1973   *The Death of White Sociology.* New York: Random House.
1974   "Black Women in Poverty." *Journal of Social and Behavioral Sciences.* 20:41-51.
1975   "Labeling Black Children: Social Psychological Implications." *Journal of Afro-American Issues.* 3:43-52.
Lammermeier, Paul J.
1973   "The Urban Black Family of the Nineteenth Century: A Study of Black Family Structure in the Ohio Valley, 1850-1880." *Journal of Marriage and the Family.* 35:440-456.
Landis, Judson.
1960   "The Trauma of Children When Parents Divorce." *Marriage and Family Living.* 22:7-13.
1963   "Social Correlates of Divorce or Non-Divorce Among The Unhappy Married." *Marriage and Family Living.* 25:178-80.
Landry, Bart, and Margaret Platt Jendrek.
1978   "Employment of Wives in Middle-Class Black Families." *Journal of Marriage and the Family.* 40(4):787-797.
Lantz, H. R.
1977   "Free Black Family at Time of United States Census Some Implications." *International Journal of Sociology of the Family.* 7(1):37-44.
Lantz, H. R., and L. Hendrix.
1978   "Black Fertility and Black Family in 19th Century—Re-Examination of the Past." *Journal of Family History.* 3(3):251-261.
Lawden, Elizabeth A., Janet L. Hoopes, Roberta G. Andrews, Katherine D. Lower, and Susan Y. Perry.
1971   *A Study of Black Adoption Families: A Comparison of a Traditional and Quasi-Adoption Program.* New York: Child Welfare League of America.
Lawrence, Margaret M.
1975   *Young Inner-City Families: Development of Ego Strength Under Stress.* New York: Behavioral Publications.

Lee, A., and E. Lee.
1959   "The Future Fertility of the American Negro." *Social Forces.*
        37:228-231.
Lewis, Diane K.
1975   "The Black Family: Socialization and Sex Roles." *Phylon.* 36:
        221-237.
Lewis, Hylan.
1955   *Blackways of Kent.* Chapel Hill: University of North Carolina
        Press.
1961   "Child-Rearing Practices Among Low-Income Families." In
        Family Service Association of America, eds., *Casework Papers.*
        New York: Family Service Association of America.
1967a   "Culture, Class and Family Life Among Low-Income Urban
        Negroes." In Arthur Ross and Herbert Hill, eds., *Employment,
        Race and Poverty.* New York: Harcourt, Brace and World.
1967b   "The Family: New Agenda, Different Rhetoric." In Child Study
        Association of America, eds., *Children of Poverty-Children of
        Affluence.* New York: Child Study Association of America.
        Pages 1-15.
1967c   "The Family: Resources for Change." In Lee Rainwater and
        William Yancey, eds., *The Moynihan Report and the Politics
        of Controversy.* Cambridge, Mass.: M.I.T. Press.
Liebow, Elliot.
1967   *Tally's Corner.* Boston: Little, Brown.
Lincoln, C. Eric.
1965   "The Absent Father Haunts the Negro Family." *New York
        Times Magazine.* 28:60.
1966   "A Look Beyond the Matriarchy." *Ebony.* 21:111-114, 116.
Linn, Margaret W., Lee Gurel, Joan Carmichael, and Patricia Weed.
1976   "Cultural Comparisons of Mothers with Large and Small
        Families." *Journal of Biosocial Science.* 8(3):293-302.
Litwak, Eugene.
1959-60 "The Use of Extended Family Groups in the Achievement
        of Social Goals: Some Policy Implications." *Social Problems.* 7:
        177-187.
Long, Larry H., and Lynne R. Heltman.
1975   "Migration and Income Differences Between Black and White
        Men in the North." *American Journal of Sociology.* 80:1391-1409.
Lopata, Helena Z.
1971   *Occupation Housewife.* New York: Oxford University Press.

Lott, Albert J., and Bernice E. Lott.
1963   *Negro and White Youth: A Psychological Study in a Boarder State Community.* New York: Holt, Rinehart and Winston.
Lourie, Norman V.
1972   "The Migration Mass." *Social Work.* 17:77-86.
Lowrie, Samuel H.
1965   "Early Marriage: Premarital Pregnancy and Associated Factors." *Journal of Marriage and the Family.* 27:48-56.
Lyman, Stanford M.
1972   *The Black American in Sociological Thought.* New York: G.P. Putnam's Sons.
Lynd, Robert S.
1964   *Knowledge For What?* New York: Grove Press.
Lystad, M. H.
1961   "Family Patterns, Achievements and Aspiration of Urban Negroes." *Sociology and Social Research.* 45:281-288.
Mack, D. E.
1974   "Power Relationship in Black Families and White Families." *Journal of Personality and Social Psychology.* 30:409-413.
Mack, Raymond W., ed.
1968   *Race, Class and Power.* New York: American Book Co.
Madison, Bernice, and Michael Shapiro.
1969   "Long-Term Foster Family Care: What Is Its Potential for Minority Group Children." *Public Welfare.* 27:167-175.
Malinowski, Bronislaw.
1927   *Sex and Repression in Savage Society.* London: K. Paul, Trench, Truover.
Manning, Seaton W.
1964   "The Changing Negro Family: Implications for the Adoption of Children." *Child Welfare.* 43:480-485.
Mathis, Arthur.
1978   "Contrasting Approaches to Study of Black Families." *Journal of Marriage and the Family.* 40:(4)667-676.
Matza, David.
1968   "The Disreputable Poor." In Reinhard Bendix and Seymour Lipset, eds., *Class, Status and Power.* New York: Free Press.
Maxwell, Joseph W.
1968   "Rural Negro Father Participation in Family Activities." *Rural Sociology.* 33:80-83.
Mayfield, G. William.
1972   "Mental Health in the Black Community." *Social Work.* 17:106-110.

McAdoo, Harriet P.
1977a "Family Therapy in the Black Community." *American Journal of Orthopsychiatry.* 47(1):75-79.
1977b "Review of Literature Related to Family Therapy in The Black Community." *Journal of Contemporary Psycho-Therapy.* 9(1):15-19.
1978   "Factors Related to Stability in Upwardly Mobile Black Families." *Journal of Marriage and the Family.* 40(4):761-776.
McAdoo, John L.
1979   "Father-Child Interaction Patterns and Self-Esteem in Black Pre-School Children." *Young Children.* 34(2):46-53.
McCarthy, J., and J. Menken.
1979   "Marriage, Remarriage, Marital Disruption and Age at 1st Birth." *Family Planning Perspective.* 11(1):21.
McCarthy, James F.
1979   "Racial Differences in the Dissolution of 1st Marriage—Results from the 1973 National Survey of Family Growth." *Popular Index.* 45(3):419-420.
McCord, J., W. McCord, and E. Thurber.
1962   "Some Effects of Paternal Absence on Male Children." *Journal of Abnormal and Social Psychology.* 64:361-369.
McLaughlin, Clara J.
1976   *Black Parents' Handbook: A Guide to Health, Pregnancy, Birth, and Child Care.* New York: Harcourt, Brace, Jovanovich.
McNair, Charles L.
1975   "The Black Family is Not a Matriarchal Family Form." *Negro Educational Review.* 26:93-100.
Meier, August, and Elliott Rudwick.
1970   *From Plantation to Ghetto.* New York: Hill and Wang.
Melton, Willie, and Darwin L. Thomas.
1976   "Instrumental and Expressive Values in Mate Selection of Black and White College Students." *Journal of Marriage and the Family.* 38(3):509-517.
Mercer, Charles V.
1967   "Interrelations Among Family Stability, Family Composition Residence and Race." *Journal of Marriage and the Family.* 29:456-460.
Merton, Robert.
1973   *The Sociology of Science.* Chicago: University of Chicago Press.
Miao, Greta.
1974   "Marital Instability and Unemployment Among Whites and Nonwhites, The Moynihan Report Revisited—Again." *Journal of Marriage and the Family.* 36:77-86.

Middleton, Russell, and Snell Putney.
1960   "Dominance in Decisions in the Family: Race and Class Differences." *American Journal of Sociology.* 65:604-609.
Miller, Kent S., and Ralph M. Dreger, eds.
1973   *Comparative Studies of Blacks and Whites in the United States.* New York: Seminar Press.
Mindel, Charles H., and R. W. Haberman.
1976   *Ethnic Families in America.* New York: Elsevier Scientific Publishing Company.
Monahan, Thomas P.
1955   "Is Childlessness Related to Family Stability?" *American Sociological Review.* 20:446-456.
1958   "Family Fugitives." *Marriage and Family Living.* 20:146-151.
Montagu, Ashley.
1974   *Man's Most Dangerous Myth: The Fallacy of Race.* 5th edition. New York: Oxford University Press.
Morris, Naomi M., and Benjamin S. Sison.
1974   "Correlates of Female Powerlessness: Parity, Method of Birth Control, Pregnancy." *Journal of Marriage and the Family.* 36: 708-713.
Mott, Frank L., et al.
1979   *Women, Work and Family: Dimensions of Change in American Society.* Lexington, Mass.: Lexington Books.
Moynihan, Daniel Patrick.
1965a   "Employment, Income, and the Ordeal of the Negro Family." *Daedalus.* 94:740-770.
1965b   *The Negro Family: The Case for National Action.* Washington, D.C.: U.S. Government Printing Office. Prepared for the U.S. Department of Labor, Office of Policy Planning and Research.
Mussen, P., and L. Distler.
1959   "Masculinity, Identification and Father-Son Relationships." *Journal of Abnormal and Social Psychology.* 59:350-356.
Myers, Lena Wright.
1974   "Mothers from Families of Orientation as Role Models for Black Women." *Northwest Journal of African and Black American Studies.* 2:(1)7-9.
Myrdal, Gunnar.
1944   *An American Dilemma.* New York: Harper Torchbooks.
Newcomb, Andrew F., and Andrew W. Collins.
1979   "Children's Comprehension of Family Role Portrayals in Televised Dramas: Effects of Socioeconomic Status, Ethnicity and Age." *Developmental Psychology Journal.* 15(4):417-423.

Nobles, Wade W.
1974a   "Africanity: Its Role in Black Families." *The Black Scholar.*
        June:12-13.
1974b   "African Root and American Fruit: The Black Family." *Journal*
        of Social and Behavioral Sciences. 20:52-64.
1976   *A Formulative and Empirical Study of Black Families.* Final Report.
        Washington, D.C.: U.S. Department of Health, Education and
        Welfare.
1978   "Toward an Empirical and Theoretical Framework for Defining
        Black Families." *Journal of Marriage and the Family.* 40(4)
        679-688.
Nobles, Wade W., and Lawford L. Goddard.
1977   "Consciousness, Adaptability and Coping Strategies: Socio-
        Economic Characteristics and Ecological Issues in Black Families.
        Western Journal of Black Studies. (2):105-113.
Nolle, Davie B.
1972   "Changes in Black Sons and Daughters: A Panel Analysis of
        Black Adolescents, Orientations Toward Their Parents." *Journal*
        of Marriage and the Family. 34:443-447.
Novak, Michael.
1977   "The Family Out of Favor." *Urban and Social Change Review.*
        10(1):3-6.
Nye, F. Ivan.
1952   "Adolescent-Parent Adjustment: Age, Sex, Sibling Number,
        Broken Homes, and Employed Mothers as Variables." *Marriage*
        and Family Living. 14:327-332.
1959a   "Child Adjustment in Broken and in Unhappy Unbroken Homes."
        Marriage and Family Living. 19:356-361.
1959b   "Employment Status of Mothers and Adjustment of Adolescent
        Children." *Marriage and Family Living.* 20:240-244.
Nye, F. Ivan, and Lois W. Hoffman, eds.
1963   *The Employed Mother in America.* Chicago: Rand McNally.
O'Kare, James.
1969   "Ethnic Mobility and The Lower Income Negro: A Socio-
        historical Perspective." *Social Problems.* 16:302-311.
Olsen, Marvin E.
1960   "Distribution of Family Responsibilities and Social Stratifications."
        Marriage and Family Living. 22:60-65.
Olson, David H.
1969   "The Measurement of Family Power by Self-Report and
        Behavioral Methods." *Journal of Marriage and the Family.*
        31:545-550.

Osofsky, Gilbert, ed.
1969   *Puttin On Ole Massa.* New York: Harper and Row.
Otto, Herbert.
1962   "What is a Strong Family?" *Marriage and Family Living.*
        24:77-89.
Otto, Luther B.
1975   "Class Status in Family Research." *Journal of Marriage and the
        Family.* 37:315-332.
Park, Robert E., and Ernest W. Burgess.
1924   *Introduction to the Science of Sociology.* Chicago: University of
        Chicago Press.
Parker, Seymour, and Robert Kleiner.
1966   "Characteristics of Negro Mothers in Single-Headed Households."
        Journal of Marriage and the Family. 28:507-513.
1969   "Social and Psychological Dimensions of the Family Role
        Performance of the Negro Male." *Journal of Marriage and the
        Family.* 31:500-506.
Parsons, Talcott, and Robert F. Bales.
1955   *Family, Socialization and Interaction Process.* New York: Free Press.
Pederson, Frank A., Judith S. Rubinstein, and Leon J. Yarrow.
1979   "Infant Development in Father Absent Families." *Journal of
        Genetic Psychology.* 135(1):51-61.
Peters, Marie.
1974   "Black Family: Perpetuating the Myths. An Analysis of Family
        Sociology Textbook Treatment of Black Families." *Family
        Coordinator.* 23:349-357.
1978   *Journal of Marriage and the Family.* Special Issue. 40(4):655-658.
1979   "Extended Family in Black Societies." *Journal of Marriage and
        the Family.* 51(4):907-910.
Phillips, Derek L.
1971   *Knowledge From What?* Chicago: Rand McNally.
Pinkney, Alphonso.
1969   "The Family." *Black Americans.* Englewood Cliffs, N.J.: Prentice-
        Hall. Pages 91-98.
Pleck, Elizabeth.
1972   "The Two-Parent Households: Black Family Structure in Late
        Nineteenth Century Boston." In Michael Gordon, ed. *The
        American Family in Socio-Historical Perspective.* New York:
        St. Martin's Press. Pages 152-178.
Pope, Hallowell.
1967   "Unwed Mothers and their Sex Partners." *Journal of Marriage
        and the Family.* 29:555-567.

1969   "Negro-White Differences in Decisions Regarding Illegitimate Children." *Journal of Marriage and the Family.* 31:756-764.

Pope, Hallowell, and Dean D. Knudsen.

1965   "Premarital Sexual Norms, The Family and Social Change." *Journal of Marriage and the Family.* 27:314-323.

Poussaint, Alvin.

1977   "Rising Suicide Rates Among Blacks." *Urban League Review.* 3(1):22-30.

Pricebonham, Sharon, and P. Skeen.

1979   "Comparison of Black and White Fathers with Implications for Parent Education." *Family Coordinator.* 28(10):53-59.

Putney, Snell, and Russell Middleton.

1960   "Effect of Husband-Wife Interaction on the Structure of Attitudes Toward Child Rearing." *Marriage and Family Living.* 22:171-173.

Queen, Stuart.

1967   *The Family in Various Cultures.* Philadelphia: Lippincott.

Radin, Norma, and Paul H. Blasser.

1965   "The Use of Parental Attitude Questionnaires with Culturally Disadvantaged Families." *Journal of Marriage and the Family.* 27:373-383.

Radin, Norma, and Constance K. Kamii.

1965   "The Child Rearing Attitudes of Disadvantaged Negro Mothers and Some Educational Implications." *Journal of Negro Education.* 34:138-146.

Rainwater, Lee.

1960   *And the Poor Get Children.* Chicago: Quadrangle Books.

1964   *Family Design: Marital Sexuality, Family Size and Contraception.* Chicago: Aldine.

1966a   "Comment on Bernard." *Journal of Marriage and the Family.* 28:442-445.

1966b   "Crucible of Identity: The Negro Lower-Class Family." *Daedalus.* 95:172-216.

1966c   "Marital Stability and Patterns of Status Variables: A Comment." *Journal of Marriage and the Family.* 28:442-446.

1966d   "Some Aspects of Lower-Class Sexual Behavior." *Journal of Social Issues.* 22:96-108.

1968   "Family and Social Pathology in the Ghetto." *Science.* 161:756-762.

1970a   *Behind Ghetto Walls: Black Family Life in a Federal Slum.* Chicago: Aldine.

1970b   "The Problem of Lower Class Culture." *Journal of Social Issues.* 26:133-148.

1970c   *Soul.* Chicago: Aldine.

Rainwater, Lee, and Gerald Handel.
1964   "Changing Family Roles in the Working Class." In Arthur B. Shostak and William Gomberg, eds., *Blue Collar World*. Englewood Cliffs, N.J.: Prentice-Hall.

Rainwater, Lee, and Marc Swartz.
1965   *The Working Class World: Identity, World View, Social Relations and Family Behavior Magazines*. Chicago: Social Research.

Rainwater, Lee, and William Yancey.
1967   *The Moynihan Report and the Politics of Controversy*. Cambridge, Mass.: M.I.T. Press.

Ramirez, Manuel, and Douglass Price-Williams.
1976   "Achievement Motivation in Children of Three Ethnic Groups in the United States." *Journal of Cross-Cultural Psychology*. 7(1):49-60.

Rawick, George P.
1972   *The American Slave: A Composite Autobiography/From Sunup to Sundown: The Making of the Black Community*. Westport, Conn.: Greenwood Press.

Real, W., ed.
1977   *Racism in America. Role Behavior and Stereotyping as Obstacles to Black Identity*. Paderborn, West Germany: Schoningh.

Reed, Fred W., and J. Richard Udry.
1973   "Female Work, Fertility and Contraceptive in a Biracial Sample." *Journal of Marriage and the Family*. 35:597-603.

Reid, Ira De A.
1940   *In a Minor Key: Negro Youth in Story and Fact*. New York: American Council on Education.

Reiner, Beatrice.
1968   "The Real World of the Teenage Negro Mother." *Child Welfare*. 47:391-396.

Reiss, Ira L.
1960   *Premarital Sexual Standards in America*. New York: Free Press.
1964   "Premarital Sexual Permissiveness Among Negroes and Whites." *American Sociological Review*. 29:688-698.
1967a   *Permissiveness*. New York: Holt, Rinehart and Winston.
1967b   *The Social Context of Premarital Sexual Permissiveness*. New York: Holt, Rinehart and Winston.

Reissman, Frank.
1964   "Low Income Culture: The Strengths of the Poor." *Journal of Marriage and the Family*. 26:417-421.
1966   "In Defense of the Negro Family." *Dissent*. 13:141-155.

1969   *Strategies Against Poverty.* New York: Random House.

Reissman, Frank, and Hermine I. Papper.

1968   *Up From Poverty.* New York: Harper and Row.

Renne, Karen S.

1970   "The Correlates of Dissatisfaction in Marriage." *Journal of Marriage and the Family.* 32:54-66.

Riegel, Robert E.

1970   *American Women.* Teaneck, N.J.: Farleigh Dickinson University Press.

Robins, Lee N., P. A. West, and B. L. Herjanic.

1975   "Arrests and Delinquency in Two Generations: A Study of Black Urban Families and their Children." *Journal of Child Psychology and Psychiatry.* 16(2):125-140.

Robins, Lee N., and E. Wish.

1977   "Childhood Deviance as a Developmental Process: A Study of 223 Urban Black Men from Birth to 18." *Social Forces.* 56(2):448-473.

Rodgers-Rose, La Frances.

1980   *The Black Woman.* Beverly Hills, Calif.: Sage.

Rodman, Hyman.

1963   "The Lower Class Value Stretch." *Social Forces.* 41:205-215.

1964   "Middle-Class Misconception about Lower-Class Families." In Arthur B. Shostak and William Gomberg, eds., *Blue Collar World.* Englewood Cliffs, N.J.: Prentice-Hall.

1965   "The Textbook World of Family Sociology." *Social Problems.* 12:445-457.

1966   "Illegitimacy in the Caribbean Social Structure: A Reconsideration." *American Sociological Review.* 31:673-683.

1968   "Family and Social Pathology in the Ghetto." *Science.* 16: 756-761.

1971   *Lower Class Families.* New York: Oxford University Press.

Rohrer, John, and Munro Edmonson.

1960   *The Eighth Generation Grows Up: Cultures and Personalities of the New Orleans Negroes.* New York: Harper and Row.

Rosaldo, Michele Z., and Louise Lamphere, eds.

1974   *Woman, Culture and Society.* Stanford, Calif.: Stanford University Press.

Rosengarten, Theodore.

1974   *All God's Dangers: The Life of Nate Shaw.* New York: Avon.

Rubin, Roger Harvey.

1976   *Matricentric Family Structure and the Self-Attitudes of Negro Children.* San Francisco: R & E Publishing Co.

1978   "Matriarchal Themes in Black Family Literature: Implications for Family Life Education." *Family Coordinator.* 27(1):33-41.

Rubinstein, Judith L., F. A. Pederson, and L. J. Yarrow.

1977   "What Happens When Mother is Away?" *Developmental Psychology.* 13(5):529-530.

Russell-Wood, A. J. R.

1978   "The Black Family in the Americas." *Societas.* 8(1):1-38.

Ryan, William.

1965   "Savage Discovery: The Moynihan Report." *The Nation.* 201:380-384.

1976   *Blaming the Victim.* Revised edition. New York: Vintage.

Safa, Helen I.

1967   *An Analysis of Upward Mobility in Low-Income Families: A Comparison of Family and Community Life Among Negro and Puerto Rican Poor.* Syracuse, N.Y.: Syracuse University Press.

Sager, C. J., T. L. Brayboy, and B. A. Waxenbery.

1970   *The Black Ghetto Family in Therapy: A Laboratory Experience.* New York: Grove Press.

Sampson, William A., and Peter Rossi.

1975   "Race and Family Social Standing." *American Sociological Review.* 40(2):201-214.

Samuels, Douglas D., and R. J. Griffore.

1977   "Ethnic Differences in Mothers' Anxiety." *Psychological Reports.* 40:1270.

Santrock, J.

1970   "Paternal Absence, Sex Typing and Identification." *Psychology.* 2:264-272.

Savage, James E., Alvis V. Adair, and Philip Friedman.

1978   "Community Social Variables Related to Black Parent Absent Families." *Journal of Marriage and the Family.* 40(4):779-785.

Scanzoni, John H.

1971   *The Black Family in Contemporary Society.* Boston: Allyn and Bacon.

1975   "Sex Roles, Economic Factors, and Marital Solidarity in Black and White Marriages." *Journal of Marriage and the Family.* 37:130-145.

Scheck, D. C., and R. Emerick.

1976   "Young Male Adolescents' Perception of Early Child-Rearing Behavior: The Differential Effects of Socioeconomic Status and Family Size." *Sociometry.* 39:39-52.

Schermerhorn, R. A.
1966   "Comment on Bernard." *Journal of Marriage and the Family.*
        28:440-442.
Schiller, Bradley R.
1973   *The Economics of Poverty and Discrimination.* Englewood Cliffs,
        N.J.: Prentice-Hall.
Schneer, Henry I., A. Perlstein, and M. Brozovsky.
1975   "Hospitalized Suicidal Adolescents: Two Generations." *Journal
        of Child Psychiatry.* 14(2):268-280.
Schulz, David A.
1969a   *Coming Up Black: Patterns of Ghetto Socialization.* Englewood
        Cliffs, N.J.: Prentice-Hall.
1969b   "Some Aspects of the Policeman's Role as It Impinges Upon
        Family Life in a Negro Ghetto." *Sociological Focus.* (September):
        63-71.
1969c   "Variations in the Father Role in Complete Families of
        the Negro Lower Class." *Social Science Quarterly.* 49:651-659.
1978   "The Role of the Boyfriend in Lower Class Negro Life."
        In Robert Staples, ed., *The Black Family: Essays and Studies.*
        Second edition. Belmont, Calif.: Wadsworth. Pages 72-76.
Schulz, David A., and Robert A. Wilson.
1973   "Some Traditional Family Variables and Their Correlations with
        Drug Use Among High School Students." *Journal of Marriage
        and the Family.* 35:628-631.
Schutz, Alfred.
1967   *Phenomenology of the Social World.* Evanston, Ill.: Northwestern
        University Press.
Schwartz, Michael.
1965   "Northern U.S. Negro Matriarchy: Status versus Authority."
        Phylon. 26:18-24.
Schweninger, Loren.
1975   "Slave Family in the Ante Bellum South." *Journal of Negro
        History.* 60:29-44.
Sciara, Frank J.
1975   "Effects of Father Absence on the Educational Achievement of
        Urban Black Children." *Child Study Journal.* 5(1):45-55.
Scott, James F.
1975   "Police Authority and the Low Income Black Family: An Area
        of Needed Research." In Lawrence E. Gary and L. P. Brown,
        eds., *Crime and Its Impact on the Black Community.* Washington,
        D.C.: Institute for Urban Affairs and Research.

Scott, John F.
1971   *Internalization of Norms.* Englewood Cliffs, N.J.: Prentice-Hall.
Scott, Joseph.
1979   "School-Age Mothers: A Look at What Is." *Black Books Bulletin.* 6(2):17-19.
1980   "Black Polygamous Family Formation." *Alternative Lifestyles.* 3(1):41-63.
Scott, P. B.
1976   "Teaching About Black Families Through Black Literature." *Journal of Home Economics.* 68:22-23.
Scott, Patricia Bell, and Patrick C. McHenry.
1977   "Some Suggestions for Teaching about Black Adolescence." *Family Coordinator.* 26(1):47-51.
Seward, Rudy R.
1978   *The American Family: A Demographic History.* Beverly Hills, Calif.: Sage.
Shade, Barbara J.
1976   "The Modal Personality of Urban Black Middle-Class Elementary School Children." *Journal of Psychology.* 92:267-275.
Shannon, Lyle W.
1975   "False Assumptions about the Determinants of Mexican-American and Negro Economic Absorption." *Sociological Quarterly.* 16(1): 3-15.
Sherman, Richard, ed.
1970   *The Negro and the City.* Englewood Cliffs, N.J.: Prentice-Hall.
Shimkin, Dmitri.
1979   *Extended Family in Black Society.* The Hague: Mouton.
Shin, E. H.
1976   "Earnings Inequality Between Black and White Males by Education, Occupation and Region." *Sociology and Social Research.* 60:161-172.
Shireman, Joan F., and Penny R. Johnson.
1976   "Single Persons as Adoptive Parents." *Social Service Review.* 50(1):103-116.
Shostak, Arthur B., and William Gomberg, eds.
1964   *Blue Collar World.* Englewood Cliffs, N.J.: Prentice-Hall.
Silberman, Charles E.
1964   *Crisis In Black and White.* New York: Vintage.
Simpson, R. L.
1962   "Parental Influence, Anticipatory Socialization and Social Mobility." *American Sociological Review.* 27:517-522.

Sims, Edward.
1978   *Black Nomads in the Urban Centers.* Washington, D.C.: University Press of America.

Sizemore, Barbara A.
1972   "Social Science and Education for a Black Identity." In James A. Banks and Jean D. Grambs, eds., *Black Self-Concept.* New York: McGraw-Hill.
1973   "Sexism and the Black Male." *Black Scholar.* 4(6-7):2-11.

Sjirmaki, John.
1964   "The Institutional Approach." In Harold T. Christensen, ed., *Handbook of Marriage and the Family.* Chicago: Rand McNally.

Sly, David.
1970   "Minority Group Status and Fertility." *American Journal of Sociology.* 76:443-450.

Smallwood, J.
1977   "Emancipation and Black Family Case Study in Texas." *Social Science.* 57(4):849-857.

Smith, Carey J.
1977   *Black-White Reproductive Behavior: An Economic Interpretation.* San Francisco: R & E Research Associates.

Smith, D. S., M. Dablin, and M. Fredberger.
1979   "Family Structure of the Older Black Population in the American South 1880 and 1900." *Sociology and Social Research.* 63(3):544-565.

Smith, Howard P., and Marcia Abrahamson.
1962   "Racial and Family Experience Correlates of Mobility Aspirations." *Journal of Negro Education.* 31:117-124.

Smith, Raymond T.
1970   "The Nuclear Family in Afro-American Kinship." *Journal of Comparative Family Studies.* 1:55-70.

Spaights, Ernest.
1973   "Some Dynamics of the Black Family." *Negro Educational Review.* 24:127-137.
1976   "Evolving Black Family in the United States, 1950-1974." *Negro Educational Review.* 27:113-128.

Stack, Carol B.
1974   *All Our Kin: Strategies for Survival in a Black Community.* New York: Harper and Row.

Stafford, J. E., K. K. Cox, and J. B. Higgenbotham.
1968   "Some Consumption Pattern Differences Between Urban Whites and Negroes." *Social Science Quarterly.* 59:619-630.

Staples, Robert.
1966   "Sex Life of Middle Class Negroes." *Sexology*. 33:86-89.
1967   "Mystique of Black Sexuality." *Liberator*. 7:8-11.
1969   "Research on the Negro Family: A Source for Family Practitioners." *The Family Coordinator*. 18:202-210.
1970a   "Educating the Black Male of Various Class Levels for Marital Roles." *Family Coordinator*. 19:164-167.
1970b   "The Myth of the Black Matriarchy." *The Black Scholar*. January-February: 9-16.
1971a   *The Black Family: Essays and Studies*. Belmont, Calif.: Wadsworth.
1971b   "Toward a Sociology of the Black Family: A Theoretical and Methodological Assessment." *Journal of Marriage and the Family*. 33:19-38.
1973a   *The Black Woman in America: Sex, Marriage and The Family*. Chicago: Nelson-Hall Publishers.
1973b   "Public Policy and the Changing Status of Black Families." *Family Coordinator*. 22:345-351.
1974a   "The Black Family in Evolutionary Perspective." *Black Scholar*. 5:2-9.
1974b   "The Black Family Revisited: A Review and a Preview." *Journal of Social and Behavioral Sciences*. 20:65-78.
1976   *Introduction to Black Sociology*. New York: McGraw-Hill.
1978a   ed., *The Black Family: Essays and Studies*. Second edition. Belmont, Calif.: Wadsworth.
1978b   "Race, Liberalism-Conservatism, and Premarital Sexual Permissiveness: A Bi-Racial Comparison." *Journal of Marriage and the Family*. 40(4):733-742.
1979   "Beyond the Black Family: The Trend Toward Singlehood." *Western Journal of Black Studies*. 3(3):150-156.
Stephens, William N.
1961   "Judgement by Social Workers on Boys and Mothers in Fatherless Families." *Journal of Genetic Psychology*. 99:59-64.
Stewart, John B.
1980   "Perspectives on Black Families From Contemporary Soul Music— The Case of Millie Jackson." *Phylon*. 41(1):57-71.
Stinnett, Nick, Sharon Talley, and James Walters.
1973   "Parent-Child Relationships of Black and White High School Students: A Comparison." *Journal of Social Psychology*. 91:349-350.
Stolz, Lois Meek.
1960   "Effects of Mothers' Employment on Children: Evidence from Research." *Child Development*. 21:749-782.

Strodbeck, Fred L.
1964   "The Poverty-Dependence Syndrome of the ADC Female-Based Negro Family." *American Journal of Orthopsychiatry.* 34:216-217.

Sudarkasa, Niara.
1975   "Exposition on the Value Premises Underlying Black Family Studies." *National Medical Association Journal.* 67:235-239.

Sussman, Marvin, and Lee Burchinal.
1962   "Kin Family Network: Unheralded Structure in Current Conceptualizations of Family Functioning." *Marriage and Family Living.* 24:231-240.

Sussman, Marvin, and H. C. Yeager, Jr.
1950   "Mate Selection Among Negro and White College Students." *Sociology and Social Research.* 35:46-49.

Swan, L. Alex.
1974   "A Methodological Critique of the Moynihan Report." *Black Scholar.* 5:18-24.

Sweet, J. R., and K. B. Thornberg.
1971   "Preschooler's Self and Social Identity within the Family Structure." *Journal of Negro Education.* 40:22-27.

Sweet, James A.
1974   "Differences in Marital Instability of the Black Population." *Phylon.* 34:323-331.

Tanner, Nancy.
1974   "Matrifocality in Indonesia and Africa and Among Black Americans." In Michele Z. Rosaldo and Louise Lamphere, eds., *Women, Culture and Society.* Stanford, Calif.: Stanford University Press.

Tausky, Curt, and William J. Wilson.
1971   "Work Attachment Among Black Men." *Phylon.* 32:23-30.

Taylor, Howard F.
1973   "Playing the Dozens with Path Analysis: Methodological Pitfalls in Jencks, et al., *Inequality.*" *Sociology of Education.* Fall: 433-450.

TenHouten, Warren D.
1970   "The Black Family: Myth and Reality." *Psychiatry.* 33:145-173.

Terrell, Francis.
1975   "Dialectical Differences Between Middle-Class Black and White Children Who Do and Do Not Associate with Lower-Class Children." *Language and Speech.* 18(1):65-73.

Thomas, Alexander, and Samuel Sillen.
1972   *Racism and Psychiatry.* New York: Brunner/Mazel.

Thomas, George B.
1974   *Young Black Adults: Liberation and Family Attitudes.* New York: Friendship Press.
Thompson, Daniel C.
1965   *The Negro Leadership Class.* Englewood Cliffs, N.J.: Prentice-Hall.
1974   *Sociology of the Black Experience.* Westport, Conn.: Greenwood Press.
Thompson, Edgar T., ed.
1939   *Race Relations and the Race Problem.* Durham, N.C.: Duke University Press.
Thorpe, Earl E.
1961   "Ante-Bellum Classes and Family Life Among Negroes." In *The Mind of the Negro: An Intellectual History of Afro-Americans.* Baton Rouge, La.: Outlieh Press.
Tietze, C., and S. Lewit.
1953   "Patterns of Family Limitation in a Rural Negro Community." *American Sociological Review.* 18:563-564.
Tobin, James.
1965   "On Improving the Economic Status of the Negro." *Daedalus.* 94:878-898.
Trader, Harriet P.
1979   "Welfare Policies and Black Families." *Social Work.* 24(6): 548-552.
Turner, C. R.
1972   "Some Theoretical and Conceptual Considerations for Black Family Studies." *Black Lines.* 2:13-27.
Turner, Ralph H.
1970   *Family Interaction.* New York: John Wiley & Sons.
Udry, J. Richard.
1967a   "Marital Instability by Race and Income Based on 1960 Census Data." *American Journal of Sociology.* 72:673-674.
1967b   "Marital Instability by Race, Sex, Education, and Occupation Using 1960 Census Data." *American Journal of Sociology.* 72:203-209.
Udry, J. Richard, Karl E. Bauman, and Charles Chase.
1971   "Skin Color, Status and Mate Selection." *American Journal of Sociology.* 87:722-733.
United States Bureau of the Census.
1973   *The Social and Economic Status of the Black Population in the United States: An Historical View, 1790-1978.* Current Population Reports, Series P-23, No. 80. Washington, D.C.: U.S. Government Printing Office.

United States Department of Commerce, Bureau of the Census.

1976   *Characteristics of the Population Below the Poverty Level: 1974.*
Washington, D.C.: U.S. Government Printing Office.

1980a   *American Families and Living Arrangements.* Special Studies.
Washington, D.C.: U.S. Government Printing Office.

1980b   *Characteristics of the Population Below the Poverty Level: 1978.*
Washington, D.C.: U.S. Government Printing Office.

1980c   *Household and Family Characteristics: March 1979.* Washington,
D.C.: U.S. Government Printing Office.

1980d   *Marital Status and Living Arrangements: March 1979.* Washington,
D.C.: U.S. Government Printing Office.

1980e   *Money Income of Families and Persons in the United States: 1978.*
Washington, D.C.: U.S. Government Printing Office.

United States Department of Justice, Bureau of Justice Statistics.

1980   *Prisoners in State and Federal Institutions on December 31, 1978.*
Washington, D.C.: U.S. Government Printing Office.

United States Department of Labor, Office of Policy Planning and
Research.

1965   *The Negro Family: The Case for National Action.* Prepared by
Daniel Patrick Moynihan. Washington, D.C.: U.S. Government
Printing Office.

Urban League.

1975   *Black Families in the 1974-75 Depression.* Washington, D.C.:
National Urban League Research Department.

Valentine, Charles A.

1968   *Culture and Poverty.* Chicago: University of Chicago Press.

Valien, Preston, and Alberta Fitzgerald.

1949   "Attitudes of the Negro Mother Toward Birth Control."
American Journal of Sociology. 55:279-283.

Ventura, Stephanie J.

1969   "Recent Trends and Differentials in Illegitimacy." *Journal of
Marriage and the Family.* 31(8):447-450.

Vincent, Clark.

1959   "Ego Involvement in Sex Relations: Implications for Research
on Illegitimacy." *American Journal of Sociology.* 65:287-296.

1961   *Unmarried Mothers.* Glencoe, Ill.: Free Press.

Vincent, Clark E., Carl M. Cochrane, and C. Allen Haney.

1969   "Familial and Generational Patterns of Illegitimacy." *Journal of
Marriage and the Family.* 31(8):136-147.

Vontress, Clemment E.

1971   "The Black Male Personality." *The Black Scholar.* 2:10-16.

Walters, James, and Ruth Connors.
1964   "Interaction of Mother and Children From Lower-Class Families." *Child Development* 35:433-440.
Weaver, Jerry L.
1977   "Policy Responses to Complex Issues: The Case of Black Infant Mortality." *Journal of Health, Politics, Policy and Law.* 1(4): 433-443.
Weems, Luther.
1974   "Black Community Research Needs: Methods, Models, and Modalities." In Lawrence Gary, ed., *Social Research and the Black Community: Selected Issues and Priorities.* Washington, D.C.: Institute for Urban Affairs and Research. Pages 25-38.
Weller, Leonard, and Elmer Luchterhand.
1969   "Comparing Interviews and Observations on Family Functioning." *Journal of Marriage and the Family.* 31:115-122.
1973   "Effects of Improved Housing on the Family Functioning of Large, Low-Income Black Families." *Social Problems.* 20(3): 382-388.
White, Joyce.
1978   "Single Motherhood." In Robert Staples, ed., *The Black Family: Essays and Studies.* Second edition. Belmont, Calif.: Wadsworth.
Whitehead, John S.
1969   *Ida's Family: Adaptations to Poverty in a Suburban Ghetto.* Yellow Springs, Ohio: Antioch College.
White House Conference on Families.
1980   Volume 1, No. 10, August.
Wilkinson, Charles B., and William A. O'Connor.
1977   "Growing up Male in a Black Single-Parent Family." *Psychiatric Annals.* 7(7):50-51, 55-59.
Wilkinson, Doris L.
1979   "Toward a Positive Frame of References for Analysis of Black Families. Selected Bibliography." *Journal of Marriage and the Family.* 40(4):707-708.
Wilkinson, Doris Y., and Ronald L. Taylor.
1970   *The Black Male in America.* Chicago: Nelson Hall.
Will, Robert, and Harold G. Vatter.
1970   *Poverty in Affluence: The Social, Political and Economic Dimensions of Poverty in the United States.* New York: Harcourt, Brace and World.
Williams, J. Allen, Jr., and Robert Stockton.
1973   "Black Family Structures and Functions: An Empirical Exami-

nation of Some Suggestions Made by Billingsley." *Journal of Marriage and the Family.* 35(1):39-49.

Willie, Charles V., ed.
1970   *The Family Life of Black People.* Columbus, Ohio: Charles E. Merrill.
1976   *A New Look at Black Families.* New York: General Hall.

Willie, Charles V., and Susan F. Greenblatt.
1978   "Four Classic Studies of Power Relationships in Black Families – Review and Look to Future." *Journal of Marriage and the Family.* 40(4):691-694.

Willie, Charles V., and Janet Weinandy.
1970   "The Structure and Composition of 'Problem' and 'Stable' Families in a Low-Income Population." In Charles V. Willie, ed., *The Family Life of Black People.* Columbus, Ohio: Charles E. Merrill.

Winter, J. Alan, ed.
1971   *The Poor: A Culture of Poverty or a Poverty of Culture?* Grand Rapids, Mich.: William B. Ermans.

Wyatt, Gail Elizabeth.
1977   "Studying the Black Mother-Child Interaction." *Young Children.* 33(1):16-22.

Young, Donald R.
1960   "The Socialization of American Minority Peoples." In David A. Goslin, *Handbook of Socialization Theory and Research.* Chicago: Rand McNally.

Young, Virginia Heyer.
1970   "Family and Childhood in a Southern Negro Community." *American Anthropologist.* 72:269-288.

Zegiob, Leslie E., and Rex Forehand.
1975   "Maternal Interactive Behavior as a Function of Race, Socioeconomic Status and Sex of the Child." *Child Development.* 4(2):564-568.

Index

About the Author

Eleanor Engram is owner and manager of Scientific & Management Research Group in San Jose, California. Her contribution entitled "Role Transition in Early Adulthood: Orientations of Young Black Women" appeared in *Contemporary Research on Black Women*, edited by La Frances R. Rose (1980), and her articles have appeared in *Black Sociologist*.